A WORLD BANK STUDY

Funding Mechanisms for Civil Society: The Experience of the AIDS Response

René Bonnel, Rosalía Rodriguez-García, Jill Olivier, and Quentin Wodon, with Sam McPherson, Kevin Orr, and Julia Ross

THE WORLD BANK
Washington, D.C.

© 2013 International Bank for Reconstruction and Development / The World Bank
1818 H Street NW, Washington DC 20433
Telephone: 202-473-1000; Internet: www.worldbank.org

Some rights reserved

1 2 3 4   16 15 14 13

World Bank Studies are published to communicate the results of the Bank's work to the development community with the least possible delay. The manuscript of this paper therefore has not been prepared in accordance with the procedures appropriate to formally edited texts.

This work is a product of the staff of The World Bank with external contributions. Note that The World Bank does not necessarily own each component of the content included in the work. The World Bank therefore does not warrant that the use of the content contained in the work will not infringe on the rights of third parties. The risk of claims resulting from such infringement rests solely with you.

The findings, interpretations, and conclusions expressed in this work do not necessarily reflect the views of The World Bank, its Board of Executive Directors, or the governments they represent. The World Bank does not guarantee the accuracy of the data included in this work. The boundaries, colors, denominations, and other information shown on any map in this work do not imply any judgment on the part of The World Bank concerning the legal status of any territory or the endorsement or acceptance of such boundaries.

Nothing herein shall constitute or be considered to be a limitation upon or waiver of the privileges and immunities of The World Bank, all of which are specifically reserved.

Rights and Permissions

This work is available under the Creative Commons Attribution 3.0 Unported license (CC BY 3.0) http://creativecommons.org/licenses/by/3.0. Under the Creative Commons Attribution license, you are free to copy, distribute, transmit, and adapt this work, including for commercial purposes, under the following conditions:

Attribution—Please cite the work as follows: Bonnel, René, Rosalía Rodriguez-Garcia, Jill Olivier, and Quentin Wodon, with Sam McPherson, Kevin Orr, and Julia Ross. 2013. *Funding Mechanisms for Civil Society: The Experience of the AIDS Response*. Washington, DC: World Bank. doi: 10.1596/978-0-8213-9779-4 License: Creative Commons Attribution CC BY 3.0

Translations—If you create a translation of this work, please add the following disclaimer along with the attribution: *This translation was not created by The World Bank and should not be considered an official World Bank translation. The World Bank shall not be liable for any content or error in this translation.*

All queries on rights and licenses should be addressed to the Office of the Publisher, The World Bank, 1818 H Street NW, Washington, DC 20433, USA; fax: 202-522-2625; e-mail: pubrights@worldbank.org.

ISBN (paper): 978-0-8213-9779-4
ISBN (electronic): 978-0-8213-9780-0
DOI: 10.1596/978-0-8213-9779-4

Library of Congress Cataloging-in-Publication Data has been requested.

Contents

Acknowledgments vii
Acronyms ix
Executive Summary xi
   Findings xii
   Conclusions and Recommendations xvii
   Notes xix
   References xx

Chapter 1   **Introduction** 1
               Methodology 2
               Terminology and Organization of the Report 3
               Note 4
               References 4

Chapter 2   **Main Results** 5
               Trends in Donor Funding 5
               Rationale for Civil Society Involvement
                  in the AIDS Response 6
               Institutional Design of the Community Response 8
               Flow of Funds from Donors 10
               Country Funding Profiles 13
               International HIV/AIDS Alliance Survey of CSOs 21
               CADRE-OSISA Survey 24
               Conclusion 25
               Notes 28
               References 28

Appendix A   **Donor Funding Flows** 31
               The World Bank's HIV/AIDS Program 31
               The Global Fund to Fight Aids, Tuberculosis, and Malaria 36
               Emerging Issues and Developments 40
               US President's Emergency Plan for AIDS
                  Relief (PEPFAR) 43

	DFID, United Kingdom	50
	Notes	55
	References	56
Appendix B	**Country Funding Profiles**	**57**
	India	57
	Kenya	62
	Peru	67
	Key Findings of Country Profiles	70
	Notes	72
	References	73
Appendix C	**Survey of CSOs Involved in AIDS Responses**	**75**
	Responding Organizations	75
	Sources of Funding	77
	Most Important Sources of Funding	79
	Dominant Sources of Funding	79
	Expenditures on HIV and AIDS Activities	79
	Opinions about Funding, CSOs, and the AIDS Response	81
	Key Findings	82
	Note	82
	References	82
Appendix D	**OSISA-CADRE Survey of CSOs Working on HIV and AIDS**	**83**
	Responding Organizations	83
	Main Sources of Funding	84
	Key Findings	86
	Notes	87
	References	87
Appendix E	**Consultative Process**	**89**

Figures

Figure 2.1: International AIDS Assistance: Trends in G8/EC, and Other Donor Government Assistance	6
Figure 2.2: Strength of CBO Engagement and HIV Knowledge in Kenya	15
Figure 2.3: CBO Density and Service Use in Rural Areas in Nigeria	17
Figure 2.4: AIDS Resources Received by CSOs and CBOs	19
Figure 2.5: Source of CBO Funding in Kenya and Nigeria (2011)	20
Figure 2.6: Proportion of Volunteers in CSOs' Workforce (2011)	21
Figure 2.7: Dominant Funding Sources for CSOs (2010)	22
Figure 2.8: Allocation of Expenditures by CSOs	23

Figure A.1: World Bank MAP's Typical Funding Flow ... 33
Figure A.2: Variations on MAP Structures in Three Countries ... 34
Figure A.3: World Bank MAP Estimated Disbursement
   (as of September 2006) ... 35
Figure A.4: Global Fund Grant Process ... 38
Figure A.5: Disbursements by Region ... 40
Figure A.6: Disbursements to CSO PRs ... 40
Figure A.7: PEPFAR Fiscal 2010 Planned Funding for Prevention,
   Treatment, and Care ... 45
Figure A.8: PEPFAR Funding Flow, October 2003 through
   September 2009 ... 48
Figure A.9: DFID Funding Flow ... 53
Figure B.1: AIDS Funding by Source ... 63
Figure B.2: Spending by Program in Kenya ... 64
Figure B.3: Community-based Organizations in Western
   and Nyanza Provinces: Sources of Funding (2010) ... 66
Figure C.1: Proportion of Volunteers in CSOs' Workforce ... 76
Figure C.2: Type of Organizations ... 76
Figure C.3: Geographic Location of CSOs ... 77
Figure C.4: Number of Institutional Donors ... 78
Figure C.5: Frequency of CSOs Receiving Funding from each Source ... 78
Figure C.6: Average Distribution of Funding by Sources ... 79
Figure C.7: Dominant Funding Sources ... 80
Figure C.8: CSO Expenditures by Activities ... 81

Tables
Table 2.1: Population Groups Reached by CSOs in Four Regions ... 8
Table 2.2: Summary of Donors' Funding of Civil Society Organizations ... 11
Table 2.3: Value of Unpaid Volunteers as a percent
   of CBOs/NGOs' Budget ... 20
Table 2.4: Frequency and Average Distribution of Annual
   Funding among CSOs (2010) ... 22
Table A.1: Funding Flows through Civil Society Principal Recipients of the
   Global Fund's HIV and AIDS Grants (February 2003–June 2010) ... 39
Table A.2: Projected US Global Health Funding (2009–14, US$ billions) ... 46
Table A.3: Estimated PEPFAR Funding for National CSOs ... 49
Table A.4: Distribution of CSO Funding by Activity Type (Fiscal 2004–06) ... 50
Table A.5: Estimated CSO Budgets with Principal or Significant
   HIV Focus ... 54
Table B.1: First- and Second-line CSO Recipients of Key AIDS
   Funding Flows ... 59
Table B.2: Spending of CBOs and National Program by Categories ... 66
Table B.3: CSO AIDS Funding in Peru from External Sources (2006–08) ... 68

Table D.1: Expenditure Levels and Types of Organizations Funding CSOs   85
Table D.2: External Financial Assistance by Type of Expenditure   85
Table D.3: Success Rates in Funding Proposals and Dependency
   on Funding   86
Table D.4: Perspectives on Budgets and Funding Security   86

Boxes
Box A.1: PEPFAR Results   44

Acknowledgments

This report was prepared under the leadership of Rosalía Rodriguez-García, Team Leader, Evaluation of the Community Response to HIV and AIDS. It has benefited from a consultative process carried out with the UK Consortium on AIDS and International Development, which included specialists, civil society organizations, and development partners. This report is based on a document and background research (including a survey of civil society-organizations working on HIV and AIDS) that was prepared by the International HIV/AIDS Alliance with the support of the following: (1) South Asia Technical Support Hub: Meera Mishra (consultant) and Shaleen Rakesh of Alliance India; (2) KANCO—Urbanus Mutuku Kioko (consultant) in Kenya; and (3) LAC Techical Support Hub, Aurora Riva Patron (consultant) in Peru, under the guidance of Sam McPherson. The report also includes funding data for community-based organizations in Nigeria and Kenya, which was obtained from the World Bank's Evaluation of the Community Response to HIV and AIDS. Additional research was carried out by Jill Olivier and Quentin Wodon at the Development Dialogue on Values and Ethics (DDVE) at the World Ba nk using data previously collected by OSISA-CADRE and graciously made available to the authors by Kevin Kelly. DDVE also conducted a literature review of donor funding for, and perceptions of, faith-based organizations working on HIV/AIDS.

The final version was prepared by René Bonnel with significant contributions from and Rosalía Rodriguez-García, Jill Olivier, NDella Njie, F. Brian Pascual, and Quentin Wodon. The authors wish to thank and acknowledge the reviewers listed in the appendix for providing useful comments and insights on previous versions of this paper. The authors would also like to acknowledge the support of David Wilson, Director of the HIV and AIDS program at the World Bank.

The opinions expressed in this paper are those of the authors and do not necessarily represent the views of the World Bank or the Executive Directors of the World Bank and the countries they represent.

Acronyms

AIDS	Acquired immune deficiency syndrome
ART	Antiretroviral therapy
CADRE	Centre for AIDS Development, Research and Evaluation
CBO	Community-based organization
CCM	Country Coordinating Mechanism
CSO	Civil society organization
DFID	Department for International Development (UK)
FB-CSO	Faith-based civil society organization
FBO	Faith-based organization
HIV	Human immunodeficiency virus
IDU	Injecting drug user
KNASA	Kenya National AIDS Spending Assessment
KNASP III	Kenya National AIDS Strategy Plan 2009/10–2012/13
MAP	Multi-country AIDS Program
MSM	Men who have sex with men
NAC	National AIDS Commissions
NACO	National AIDS Control Organization (India)
NGO	Nongovernmental organization
NASA	National AIDS Spending Assessment
OED	Operations Evaluation Department
OSISA	Open Society Initiative of Southern Africa
OVC	Orphans and vulnerable children
PEPFAR	President's Emergency Plan for AIDS Relief (US)
PLHIV	Person or people living with HIV
PLWHA	People living with HIV and AIDS

PMTCT	Prevention of mother-to-child transmission
PPA	Partnership Programme Arrangement
PR	Principal Recipients (Global Fund)
RE	Religious entity
S-CSO	Secular civil society organization
TB	Tuberculosis
TOWA	Total War on AIDS (World Bank AIDS project)
UN	United Nations
UNAIDS	Joint United Nations Programme on HIV/AIDS
UNDP	United Nations Development Programme
VCT	Voluntary counseling and testing
WHO	World Health Organization

Executive Summary

How resources are being used to fund the community response to human immunodeficiency virus (HIV) and acquired immune deficiency syndrome (AIDS) is of considerable interest to the donor community and governments. In the past decade, international funding for the HIV and AIDS response provided by governments rose from about US$1 billion to US$8.7 billion and donors increasingly shifted their financial support toward funding community responses to this epidemic. Yet little is known about the global magnitude of these resource flows and how funding is allocated among HIV and AIDS activities and services. Although some studies have been carried out to gather information on the community response by civil society organizations (CSOs),[1] most of them provide only partial information limited to a specific intervention (for example, orphan support) or specific local communities. To address this knowledge gap, the report attempts to answer the following questions:

- How large is donor funding for community-based interventions that are run by either large nongovernmental organizations (NGOs) or smaller community-based organizations (CBOs)?
- How do the funds reach various types of CSOs?
- What are CSOs' other sources of funding, and to what extent are the CSOs dependent on donor funding?
- How are these funds used for by CSOs?
- Are there differences among different types of CSOs working on HIV and AIDS?

Information for the report came from six sources: (1) analysis of the funding provided by the most important donors; (2) country funding profiles (India, Kenya, Nigeria, and Peru); (3) an evaluation of the community response to HIV and AIDS that provided data on the funding and use of funds by CBOs in Nigeria and Kenya; (4) survey of 146 CSOs worldwide by the International HIV/AIDS Alliance; (5) analysis of Open Society Initiative of Southern Africa–Centre for AIDS Development, Research and Evaluation (OSISA–CADRE) survey of CSOs; and (6) review of the literature.

These sources provide a rich source of information on the funding environment within which CSOs operate. They help document how the funding provided by donors has become an important factor in shaping the activities of many CSOs and the challenges faced by the smaller NGOs and CBOs in mobilizing funding.

Findings

The programs implemented by the four largest donors reflect a fundamental trade-off.[2] This trade-off is between country ownership, achieving quick results, and rapid disbursement of funds versus a longer process of capacity and institution building, which would entail slower disbursement of funds. Different donors are taking different approaches, and these influence how they design channels for disbursing funds.

- **The U.S. President's Emergency Plan for AIDS Relief** (PEPFAR) was designed as an emergency response to the HIV epidemic with the objective of achieving results quickly and within a short time period. Achieving measurable results and meeting the accounting requirements set by the Congress took precedence over other objectives. This approach meant that the implementing institutions had to be large consulting firms or international NGOs with a proven record and that interventions would be done through an institutional structure separate from the countries' own systems and would not primarily contribute to building national systems for delivering HIV and AIDS services.
- **The Global Fund to Fight AIDS, Tuberculosis and Malaria** (Global Fund) was established with the goal of funding proposals developed and implemented by countries' recipients. Country ownership of the programs was the most important objective in this design. Such a design made it possible to use national actors for implementing the selected programs, but the effort faced problems in reaching small NGOs which lacked capacity to implement and monitor programs on a large scale and when governance issues arose.
- **The World Bank's HIV/AIDS Program** adopted a unique approach when it was launched in 2000.
  - The Multi-Country HIV/AIDS Program (MAP) was the first large international effort to scale-up national responses by funding a multi-sectoral response that included CSOs. As there was little national capacity at that time, priority was given to institution building, especially in Africa. This design contributed to building capacity, but it also encountered implementation bottlenecks and slow disbursement of funds when the program became entangled in national bureaucratic processes.
  - HIV and AIDS projects were also implemented in Latin America, Asia, and Eastern Europe with a similar focus on funding the community response. In India, for instance, the World Bank HIV and AIDS project helped to develop

a strategy focused on delivering preventive interventions by funding small NGOs and CBOs through performance-based contracting.
- **The UK Department for International Development (DFID)** followed an approach that combined several characteristics of other programs, including some that became drawbacks. It disbursed funds through a limited number of large NGOs and agencies to achieve specific targets, but it also created country-level channels for funding smaller national CSOs and building up national capacity.

The funding provided to CSOs has become substantial. In total, the four donors most actively involved in the AIDS response have provided, on average, at least US$690 million a year for all CSOs (NGOs, CBOs, and FBOs) during the 2003–09 period. Part of this funding "directly" reached large national CSOs. The data available from PEPFAR, DFID, and the Global Fund's database provided information on such funding. In addition, smaller NGOs and CBOs "indirectly" accessed donor funding transmitted through various channels provided by international and national NGOs, foundations and charities, government channels, and donor-pooled funds. The information available from PEPFAR and DFID did not reveal the amount of donor funding that would be transmitted through these national funding channels.[3] If this "indirect" funding is taken into account, it is likely that the total funding available for the community response would be higher.

Funding has increased substantially. Information from the CADRE—OSISA survey of 400 CSOs in Southern Africa (Birdsall and Kelly 2007) showed that the average level of spending was three times higher in 2006 than in 2001. Since then, further increases have taken place, especially as a result of the greater focus of the Global Fund on CSOs.

Only a small share of international resources trickles down to local communities. On average, large national and international CSOs receive the largest share (30–50 percent) while CBOs receive little.

- In Kenya, CSOs received 32 percent of the total HIV and AIDS funding, but only 2 percent was disbursed to CBOs according to the Kenya National AIDS Spending Assessment (KANASA) (Kenya 2009). Information provided by the Evaluation of the Community Response (World Bank 2011a) indicates that the average CBO budget amounted to US$15,000 in the eight communities that were surveyed in Western Kenya. This situation is, however, changing as a result of various initiatives. On one hand, the 2009 Kenya National AIDS Strategy reinforced the importance attached by government to community-based programs. On the other hand, CBOs have been able to access various sources of financing, including donor funding. In addition, recent evidence shows that the funding under the recent World Bank HIV and AIDS project (TOWA) is reaching small CBOs. By August 2010 over 4,000 CBOs received support amounting to US$3,500 on average.

- In Nigeria, CSOs received about 51 percent of the total funding for HIV (Nigeria 2010).[4] However, according to the National AIDS Spending Assessment (NASA) for 2008, CBOs' funding amounted to only 1.5 percent of total funding (US$395 million). As was the case in Kenya, the Evaluation of the Community Response found that the average CBO budget was small (US$17,000 on average) (World Bank 2011b).
- In Peru, funding for all CSOs amounted to 30 percent of national HIV and AIDS spending. However, about 70 percent of this funding was received by five organizations (US$1.4 million each on average) while 21 CSOs shared the rest (US$140,000 per CSO on average).
- India's funding of CSOs is relatively large, amounting to at least 27 percent of the funding available for HIV and AIDS, which reflects the substantial commitment of government and various donors in supporting the community response.

CBOs are, however, able to supplement international aid with other sources of funding. Information provided by country studies of CBO funding show that national funding channels have helped even an uneven playing field where large CSOs were the main beneficiaries of international aid.

- National funding channels have made it possible for CBOs to mobilize funding that otherwise they might not have been able to access directly. In Nigeria, for instance, the surveyed CBOs indicated that 58 percent of their budget came from foundations and charities, NGOs (national and international), and the Nigerian government. In Kenya, these same sources provided 51 percent of the surveyed CBOs' budgets.
- Volunteers are a key resource for CBOs. CBOs employ a large number of volunteers: 21 per CBO in Kenya and 51 per CBO in Nigeria. A substantial number of volunteers are currently unpaid. Estimating the value of these volunteers indicate that they increase CBOs' budget by 40 percent in Kenya and 31 percent in Nigeria. In Zimbabwe, the Evaluation of the Community Response found even greater percentage increase in NGO resources due to unpaid volunteers (69 percent) (Katietek 2012).
- However, the surveyed CBOs in Kenya and Nigeria remained heavily dependent on direct external funding. In Kenya, funding provided directly by donors to small CBOs amounted to 46 percent of CBOs' resources. In Nigeria, the corresponding percentage was 33 percent. In both cases, the dependence on external financing was higher as some of the funds provided through national funding channels were also provided by external donors.

The four country studies (India, Kenya, Nigeria, and Peru) highlighted the institutional heterogeneity of CSOs. At the national level, large international or national NGOs and FBOs have a formal and organized institutional structure. In contrast, CBOs have a much less formal structure and work with local communities. In India, for instance, CBOs often work in communities that are most at risk for HIV, while NGOs are larger organizations which often struggle in trying to reach hidden, marginalized, and stigmatized communities and do not necessarily represent the communities they work *for* rather than *with*.

The country studies presented sharp differences in terms of the involvement of CSOs and their role. At the national level, large international and national CSOs have been the main recipients of international aid due to their ability to implement projects and meet donors' reporting requirements (financial reporting, monitoring results, and providing fiduciary control) as well as their capacity to disburse funds quickly. In these cases CSOs represent a *substitute for* rather than a *complement to* government funding channels.

Small NGOs and CBOs tend to provide a complementary role to government functions, especially when it is the result of deliberate government policy decision based on the acknowledgment that small NGOs and CBOs are best placed to deliver specific HIV and AIDS services. However, their ability to play this role is limited by their weak capacity to implement projects and meet requirements of funding channels. In all four countries (India, Kenya, Nigeria, and Peru) the NGOs' and CBOs' allocation of funding for HIV and AIDS activities was markedly different from the national response.

- India has a long tradition of CSOs operating at various levels (nation, state, and local communities). Due to the importance of reaching high-risk groups for controlling the HIV epidemic, small NGOs and CBOs are at the core of the country HIV and AIDS response. They have become implementers of interventions targeting high-risk communities as a result of a deliberate government decision to channel funding to these organizations and to provide them with training. Two-thirds of the investment provided by the pooling partners—DFID, World Bank, and government—finance targeted interventions for the prevention of HIV among most at-risk populations by contracting with NGOs and CBOs to implement the program.
- Kenya has a long history of CSOs being involved in the HIV and AIDS response at the community level. Their role was confirmed by the evaluation of the community response to HIV and AIDS in Kenya (World Bank 2011a), which showed that CBOs provided services that were complementary to the government. Government HIV and AIDS spending was dominated by treatment and care (55 percent of national spending) with few resources for impact mitigation (8 percent) (Nigeria 2010). In contrast, the surveyed CBOs had a different structure of spending: 29 percent was spent for impact mitigation and only 15 percent for treatment and care (World Bank 2011a).[5]
- Nigeria's CBOs have emerged as a vital part of the response to HIV and AIDS, especially after the democratization process that started in 1999. Expansion of their role was facilitated by increased donor funding reaching them. According to the evaluation of the community response to HIV and AIDS in Nigeria, surveyed CBOs spent their resources nearly equally on prevention (25 percent),

treatment and care (23 percent), and mitigation of impact (23 percent) (World Bank 2011b).[6] At the national level, treatment and care was the largest category (48 percent), followed by program management (30 percent) and prevention (15 percent) (Nigeria 2010). CBOs' activities were particularly important in rural areas, where access to government services was more difficult.
- The involvement of Peru's CSOs in HIV and AIDS is recent, but they played a crucial role. CSOs were active in areas where few government services were available. One-third of CSO projects are targeted to most-at-risk population groups—transgender people, men who have sex with men (MSM), and sex workers—who have not been the focus of governmental prevention activities.

The survey of CSOs carried out by the International HIV/AIDS Alliance provided further support for the evidence gathered by the country studies. Respondents from 146 CSOs (mainly small NGOs and CBOs) indicated the following:

- **Their activities are mainly focused on prevention** (42 percent of CSOs' expenditures). Care and support represented almost a fifth of annual expenditure as did activities aimed at improving the enabling environment. Treatment accounted for only 15 percent of expenditures (mostly spent on treatment adherence), while impact mitigation amounted to only 6 percent of expenditures.
- **They received various sources of funding.** Respondents indicated that while the Global Fund was their most important source, providing 21 percent of their revenues, they also relied on four other channels, which represented nearly the same amount of funding: foundations and charities (15 percent), private fund-raising (16 percent), international assistance (16 percent), and other official sources (16 percent).
- **The survey highlighted the dependence of many CSOs on external funding.** One-quarter of the CSOs indicated that the Global Fund, PEPFAR, and DFID provided more than half of their resources. In the current context of declining donor funding for HIV and AIDS, there are questions about whether those CSOs will disappear or whether they could be sustained through other resources so that their experience is not lost.
- **Respondent CSOs also indicated several shortcomings.** Nearly three-quarters of the respondents mentioned that more funding is needed for activities reaching vulnerable and most-at-risk populations. A majority of CSOs also mentioned that the quality of the funding does not allow them to provide what is needed at the community level and that they do not have access to technical assistance.

Current evidence shows that small NGOs and CBOs can deliver results (World Bank 2013). The evaluation of community responses in seven countries (Burkina Faso, India, Kenya, Lesotho, Nigeria, Senegal, and Zimbabwe) found evidence that depending on the country context and service delivery mechanisms, community responses can improve knowledge and behavior, increase the use of services, affect the outcomes of social processes, and impact HIV incidence and other health outcomes. The evaluation also revealed cases where the interventions of NGOs/CBOs did not generate tangible results (both quantitative and qualitative), especially when they were interventions that had been shown to be ineffective or when they duplicated the services already provided by government and at a scale that was too small to be cost-effective. In most cases, results were country-specific, suggesting that a one-size fits all design of community responses is not appropriate. However, the evaluation shows that investments in community responses have generated results which contribute to the desired outcomes of the global response to AIDS.

Conclusions and Recommendations

The evidence gathered through the analysis of the four largest donors' databases, the three country studies and the information gathered by the evaluation of the community response to HIV and the survey of CSOs, make it possible to answer the five questions that were initially raised.

- **How large is donor funding for community-based interventions that are run by either large NGOs or smaller CBOs?** The current evidence is that the available funding for the community response is certainly large at the national level (at least US$690 million per year), but much smaller at the community level. On average the annual budget of the surveyed CBOs amounted to US$15,000 in Kenya and US$17,000 in Nigeria.
- **How do the funds reach various types of CSOs?** The available data showed that large national and international NGOs are the main recipients of donor aid. However, the country studies revealed the importance of national funding mechanisms that allow small NGOs and CBOs to access donor funding indirectly as well as government assistance.
- **What are the CSOs' other sources of funding and to what extent are CSOs dependent on donor funding?** National funding sources, including fund raising, foundations and charities have become important for small NGOs and CBOs. In addition, CBOs mobilize substantial resources in the form of unpaid volunteers. However, CSOs as a group remain heavily dependent on external funding: the online survey of 146 CSOs indicated that donor funding amounted to 47 percent of their incomes.
- **How are these funds used by CSOs?** Both the country studies and the survey of CSOs showed that CSOs play a complementary role to the national HIV and AIDS response. However, the high percentage of the surveyed CSOs that mentioned that prevention services to high-risk groups were insufficient also suggests that too much may be spent on prevention for the general population (including information and education activities) and not enough on more targeted interventions.

- **Are there differences among different types of CSOs?** The answer is clearly yes. At the national level, large NGOS and FBOs rely on professional staff, and they have the capacity to mobilize international funding and implement projects. While these organizations may work *for* local communities by delivering HIV and AIDS services, they do not necessarily work *with* local communities. This is the role that CBOs play, which enables them to rely on volunteers for their work.

Overall, small NGOs and CBOs represent a largely untapped potential for helping reverse the course and the impact of the HIV epidemic. Tapping this potential has been greatly facilitated by the establishment of various funding channels. However, getting the money to where it is needed is only part of what is required. If many of the CSOs are to remain or become effective contributors to the national AIDS response, much greater attention has to be given to the following:

1. Identifying areas for CBO interventions that are in line with the National Strategic Plan
2. Formulating national standards for providing services with implementation manuals that describe the interventions to be implemented
3. Encouraging government ministries, particularly health ministries, to enter into partnership with CBOs, especially for reaching minority groups and households at the community level and providing them with access to health and social services
4. Implementing performance-based contracting
5. Providing small NGOs and CBOs with access to an expanded source of technical training
6. Ensuring that the community response to HIV and AIDS remains sustainable over the long-term.

Focusing the activities of CSOs on effective interventions remains a challenge. The Evaluation of the Community Response to HIV (World Bank 2013) showed areas where CBOs made an impact, but it also found areas where CBOs activities did not seem to have an impact. In an environment where donor funding for HIV and AIDS is likely to become much scarcer, there is a need to examine much more closely the allocation of funding across activities and the manner in which interventions are implemented. Performance-based contracting is part of the solution for increasing effectiveness, but in addition, a more systematic provision of technical assistance is necessary.

The need for increased coordination and partnership is clearly acknowledged by both donors and national governments, but it entails higher coordination costs. Currently various institutional structures have been created to coordinate activities at the national level, but much fewer exist at the local level where the needs are perhaps greater. The examples from the country studies show some of the institutional models that are currently implemented:

- **Large umbrella organizations**: In Peru, CSOs have organized themselves under several umbrella organizations clustered around thematic priorities. Under this structure, CSOs mobilize funding from the Global Fund and channel these funds to lower levels. At the lowest level, CBOs are contracted by larger CSOs to carry out specific tasks, but the funding and the accounting are done by the larger CSOs.
- **National funding scheme**: In India, the World Bank, DFID and government have pooled their resources to support a national funding scheme that is reaching small NGOs and CBOs. Under India's third National AIDS Control Program (NACP III), there is now an increased focus on shifting the implementation of prevention interventions to NGOs/CBOs that work with most-at-risk communities and providing their organizations with technical assistance.
- **Partnership between CBOs and government ministries**: In Kenya, for example, the Ministry of Health is providing training to the volunteers employed by CBOs, which helps them provide more effective services, including referrals to other services provided by the Ministry of Health.

The rapid growth of CSOs is remarkable. It occurred in response to increased funding and to the specific needs of communities. Given these needs, it is important that these organizations are not neglected in the current increased scarcity of funding. Sustaining community responses may not require much additional funding. Furthermore, substantial increase in funding to these organizations, many of which are informal and faith-based, may drastically adversely affect their nature and function. However, strengthening CBOs' most important resource, namely their volunteers, is crucial for the long-term sustainability of community responses. This may require a formal recognition of the role played by volunteers (UK Consortium on AIDS and International Development 2010).

Notes

1. The term CSO as used here is inclusive of community-based organizations, nongovernmental organizations (NGOs), and faith-based organizations (FBOs).
2. Together, these four donors (the U.S. President's Emergency Plan for AIDS Relief, the Global Fund to Fight AIDS, Tuberculosis and Malaria, the World Bank, and the UK Department for International Development) account for more than 80 percent of the funding provided by donor governments (Kaiser 2011).
3. It is only in the case of the World Bank that an internal survey of funding provided information on the total amount reaching small NGOs and CBOs.
4. This amount is estimated from the 2008 amount received by the "private sector nonprofit providers" and excluding funding for hospitals.

5. Twenty-five CBOs were interviewed in the eight communities that were the focus of the evaluation of the community response.
6. In total, some 45 CBOs were interviewed in the six regions of Nigeria and the Federal Control Territory.

References

Birdsall, K., and K. Kelly. 2007. *Pioneers, Partners, Providers: The Dynamics of Civil Society and AIDS Funding in Southern Africa.* Johannesburg: Centre for AIDS Development, Research and Evaluation CADRE/Open Society Initiative for Southern Africa.

Kaiser. 2011. *Financing the Response to AIDS in Low-and middle-income Countries: International Assistance from the G8, European Commission and Other Donor Governments in 2009.* Menlo Park, CA: Henry Kaiser Family Foundation.

Kenya. 2009. "Kenya National AIDS Spending Assessment. Report for the Financial Years 2006/07 and 2007/08." Nairobi, Kenya: Kenya National AIDS Control Council.

Nigeria. 2010. "National AIDS Spending Assessment (NASA) for the Period 2007–2008." *Flow and Level of Resources and Expenditures of the National HIV and AIDS Response.* Abuja, Nigeria: National Agency for the Control of AIDS (NACA).

UK Consortium on AIDS and International Development. 2010. "A Roadmap to Universal Access by 2015." Summary Report of the International Conference: HIV Care & Support London, United Kingdom.

World Bank. 2011a. Riehman, K., B. Manteuffel, B. Kakietek, J. Fruh, P. Kizito, L. Vane, R. Rodriguez-Garcia, R., Bonnel, N. N'Jie, K. Bigmore, and W. Ikua. *Effects of the Community Response to HIV and AIDS in Kenya.* Washington, DC: World Bank.

———. 2011b. Idoko J. O., J. Anenih, A. Akinrogunde, S. A. Gar, I. Jalingo, T. O. Ojogun, D. Fasiku, B. Ibrahim, S. M. O. Unogu, J. Kakietek, T. Gebreselassie, B. Manteuffel, A. Krivelyova, S. Bausche, J. Fruh, R. Rodriguez-Garcia, R. Bonnel, N. N'Jie, M. O'Dwyer, and F. A. Akala. *Effects of the Community Response to HIV and AIDS in Nigeria.* Washington, DC: World Bank.

———. 2013. Rodriguez-Garcia, R., R. Bonnel, D. Wilson, N. N'Jie. *Investing in Communities Achieves Results. Findings from an Evaluation of Community Responses to HIV and AIDS.* Washington, DC: World Bank.

Katietek, J. 2012. *Flow of Resources in Community-Based Organizations in Kenya, Nigeria and Zimbabwe.* Washington, DC: World Bank.

CHAPTER 1

Introduction

Support for community responses can be provided through a variety of mechanisms that include the following:

1. Basic services funded by the central or local governments (for example, education, primary health care, and so on)
2. Funding provided by foundations, philanthropic organizations, faith-based groups, and the private sector
3. Unpaid work provided by local support groups, such as that mobilized by congregations and other community groups
4. Bilateral and multilateral donors' international assistance, whether this assistance is provided directly to civil service organizations (CSOs) or indirectly through large international CSOs, governments, or other mechanisms
5. Formal and informal safety nets that tend to reach individuals, but may also include community components or may facilitate local community responses.

This report is not intended to describe in detail how funds are provided through all of these sources, nor is it meant to analyze how funding for HIV and AIDS might have affected the health sector, as these have been already analyzed in various publications (Shiffman 2008). Instead, it focuses on retracing how the flow of international assistance from the main donor governments reaches CSOs that are operating in the countries affected by the HIV epidemic.

International AIDS support comes from a variety of donors. About 80 percent of the international funding for the global AIDS response comes, however, from four sources, namely the U.S. Government; the UK Government; the Global Fund to Fight AIDS, Tuberculosis and Malaria; and the World Bank (Kaiser 2010). For this reason, the report focuses in large part on the funding provided by these four sources. Large philanthropic foundations may also finance the HIV and AIDS response in local communities, but they are not included in this report due to difficulties in tracing their funding. The available evidence (UNAIDS 2010) suggests that philanthropic organizations provide about US$500 million per year for the AIDS response, but a large share of this funding is allocated to groups and activities in the United States.

Funding channels have become extremely complex, with institutions receiving funding from several channels and using these monies to fund different activities and smaller organizations. Because complex funding structures are often replicated at different levels, it is difficult to trace the disbursement of funds all the way down to the community level. But by analyzing the various sources of information compiled for this report, the main funding flows from donors to countries can be identified while analysis of community-based organizations (CBO) budgets provide information on the funding they receive.

Methodology

Six sources of information were used for the report:

- **Donor sources:** Mapping and descriptions of financial flows were carried out for the most important donors, namely, the US President's Emergency Plan for AIDS Relief; the Global Fund to Fight AIDS, Tuberculosis and Malaria; the World Bank; and the UK DFID.
- **Country funding profiles:** Country profiles of AIDS and civil society funding were developed for Kenya, Nigeria, India, and Peru. Information gathered was based on available data, as well as interviews with representatives from civil society, government, and the donor community.
- **Evaluation of the community response to HIV and AIDS (World Bank 2013):** The evaluation provided data on the funding and use of funds by CBOs in Kenya, Nigeria and Zimbabwe.
- **A global survey of CSOs involved in the HIV/AIDS response and implemented by the International HIV/AIDS Alliance:** 146 CSOs provided information on their allocation and sources of funding. Most of the respondents were small CBOs.
- **A second survey of CSOs working on HIV and AIDS and implemented by CADRE–OSISA:** The survey represented close to 400 CSOs from six southern African countries, with detailed information provided on funding and programs.
- **A review of the literature:** The review considered the overall evidence on funding for CBOs working on HIV and AIDS.

Each source provided partial information on the flow and allocation of funds. Taken together, these sources provide both a top-down picture (how funds flow from donors to countries) and a bottom-up picture (how local organizations are funded at the community level). By triangulating these sources, the report provides a new picture of the flow and allocation of funds at community levels.

Terminology and Organization of the Report

As a result of the increased demand for CSO services and expansion in their funding, CSOs have become a mainstay of the AIDS response. Historically, CSOs have been perceived as a group of altruistic, and often informal, organizations that are dedicated to providing services to people who would not otherwise be able to afford them, or have access to them. CSOs have also taken on the role of pioneers by implementing innovative approaches in some areas, including testing new approaches for delivering services. In the past decade, a number of more professional CSOs have become major actors in the AIDS response, often delivering substantial services and products to the population—such as the distribution of condoms or the provision of care, either directly or through smaller organizations.

As a result of their different roles, CSOs exist in many forms, ranging from support groups or associations of mainly volunteer workers to larger CSOs (Taylor 2010).[1] In this report, the term CSO references the following three types of CSOs:

- CBOs: Organizations that operate mostly in one community at a time, often informally
- Non-governmental organizations (NGOs): Organizations that work in more than one community at a time and cover part of the country
- Faith-based organizations (FBOs): Organizations that tend to be connected formally or informally to a religious movement, or have a faith-based orientation (they may be CBOs or NGOs).

Communities can be described in at least two different ways: culturally and geographically, or a combination of both (Rodriguez-García *et al.* 2011).

- A community can be defined as sharing a cultural identity. For instance, United Nations (UN 2003) defines a community as "a group of people who have something in common and will act together in their common interest." This definition would cover such groups as people living with HIV (PLHIV), MSM, and sex workers.
- A community can also refer to a geographic place. In this sense, a community refers to a specific group of people who live in a common geographical area, share a common culture, are arranged in a social structure, and exhibit some awareness of their identity as a group (UNAIDS 1999). In this report, the term *community response* refers to both types of communities.

The following chapter provides an overview of the main results of the report. Appendixes provide a more detailed description of key results from the analysis and include information on the funding channels from donors to

CSOs, the allocation of funds by CSOs across HIV and AIDS services and programs, the allocation of funds in three countries and the results from two surveys of CSOs.

Note

1. Taylor (2010) describe the different forms of structures involved in the community response for vulnerable children and what are they best placed to do.

References

Kaiser. 2010. *Financing the Response to AIDS in Low-and Middle-income Countries: International Assistance from the G8, European Commission and Other Donor Governments in 2009.* Menlo Park, CA: Henry Kaiser Family Foundation.

Rodriguez-García, R., R. Bonnel, N. Njie, J. Oliver, B. Pascual, and Q. Wodon. 2011. "Analyzing Community Responses to HIV and AIDS: Operational Framework and Typology." Policy Research Working Papers no. 5532, World Bank, Washington, DC.

Shiffman, J. 2008. "Has Donor Prioritization of HIV/AIDS Displaced Aid for Other Health Issues?" *Health Policy and Planning* 23 (2): 95–100.

Taylor, N. 2010. "The Different Forms of Structures Involved in the Community Response for Vulnerable Children, and What Are They Best Placed to Do." *Vulnerable Children and Youth Studies* 5 (S1): 7–18.

UN (United Nations). 2003. *Community Realities and Responses to HIV/AIDS in Sub-Saharan Africa.* New York: United Nations.

UNAIDS (Joint United Nations Programme on HIV/AIDS). 1999. "A Review of Household and Community Responses to the HIV/AIDS Epidemic in the Rural Areas of Sub-Saharan Africa." UNAIDS Best Practice Collection, UNAIDS, Geneva.

———. 2010. *What Countries Need; Investments Needed for 2010 Targets.* Geneva: UNAIDS.

CHAPTER 2

Main Results

Trends in Donor Funding

In the late 1990s, there was growing recognition that the HIV epidemic was exceptional and, as such, needed an exceptional response. This recognition led to the following initiatives:

- The launch in 2000 of the World Bank Multi-country AIDS Program (MAP), with an initial commitment of over US$500 million, later extended to US$1 billion for the AIDS response in Africa. This initiative was followed by further HIV and AIDS projects in other parts of the world. In total, US$2.5 billion were committed during the 1989–2010 period.
- The 2001 United Nations General Assembly Special Session on HIV/AIDS, which helped galvanize civil society and political leaders in mobilizing new funding.
- The 2002 creation of the Global Fund to Fight AIDS, Tuberculosis and Malaria, which was established with the explicit objective of becoming the main financing institution for mobilizing and disbursing AIDS funding. By December 2010, US$7.3 billion had been disbursed for HIV and AIDS.
- The 2003 launch of the (PEPFAR) by the United States, with an initial pledge of US$15 billion to be provided to 15 priority countries.
- The United Kingdom's 2004 AIDS strategy, which committed the government to spending about US$2.5 billion during three years. As a result, its HIV and AIDS budget went from £270 million in 2002/03 to £1.5 billion in 2007.

These initiatives helped build the global AIDS response. Funding for the HIV and AIDS response increased at an unprecedented rate from about US$1.2 billion in 2002 to an estimated US$16.8 billion in 2011 (UNAIDS 2012). A key reason for this increase was the international donor community's response. Donor commitments from high-income countries rose from US$1.6 billion in 2002 to US$8.7 billion in 2008 (figure 2.1). Since then, commitments have remained at about the same level. Domestic expenditures by both households and the governments of the affected countries also rose

Figure 2.1 International AIDS Assistance: Trends in G8/EC, and Other Donor Government Assistance

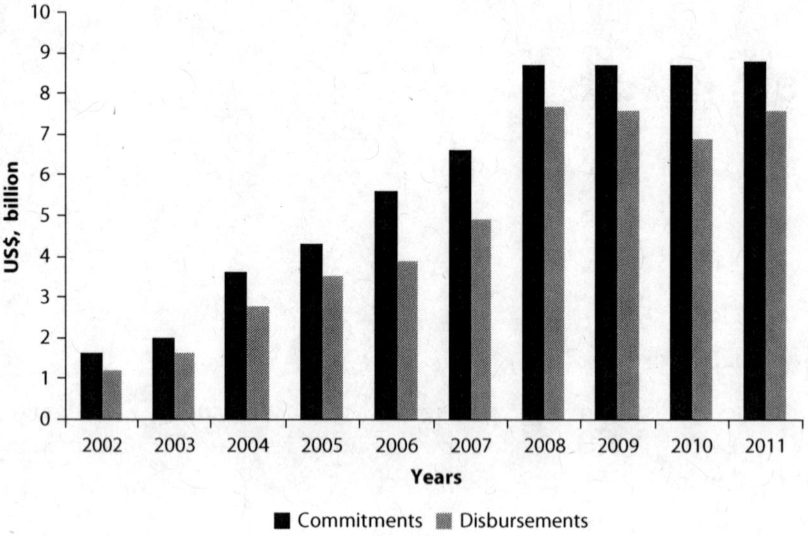

Source: Kaiser 2012.

rapidly. By 2008, these categories represented the largest share of the total AIDS response budget (52 percent).

Rationale for Civil Society Involvement in the AIDS Response

Never before had such a large amount of resources been made available for the planning, implementation, and scaling-up of HIV and AIDS initiatives at the community level. The reasons for such a dramatic strategic shift included the following:

1. A belief that small NGOs and CBOs might be able to "engineer" changes in knowledge and behavior at the local level, as the factors that influence the norms and practice of sexual behavior are more likely to be better understood by CBOs than by public sector entities
2. A desire to provide services to hard-to-reach population groups, although it was recognized that many NGOs and CBOs were insufficiently prepared to work with drug users, MSMs, and sex workers
3. A hope that CSOs might be able to implement innovative approaches that would have larger positive impacts.

Knowledge and behavior changes: In the late 1990s, there was an increased recognition that what was commonly referred to as "Community Driven

Development" could be successfully applied in the case of the AIDS response (Dongier et al. 2001). It was felt that strengthening the community response would lead to changes in knowledge, behavior, utilization of HIV services, and reduction in HIV incidence (DANIDA 2005; Delion 2004). A key ingredient of this view was the observation that, in contexts where community norms matter for individual behavior, changes in individual behavior are best attained by modifying the social norms and values of communities. This task was one that CBOs were thought to be well placed to achieve. In addition, many observers felt that the engagement of CBOs would provide added benefits by empowering communities, mobilizing political support, contributing to democratic pluralism, and developing both local ownership and longer-term sustainability (World Bank 2003).

Reaching the community level and priority populations: Another common rationale for funding CSOs is that they are believed to be well positioned to reach the people most affected by a particular challenge, such as vulnerable populations and those in remote communities, because they have strong links with, or are composed of, marginalized and hard-to-reach populations, and they may have greater expertise than others in understanding and responding to the needs of these populations (Birdsall and Kelly 2007; Drew and Attawell 2007; Homedes and Ugalde 2006; International HIV/AIDS Alliance 2007; ITPC 2008; Middleton-Lee 2007; Noack and Campioni 2006; Sidaction, UNAIDS, and WHO 2005; World Bank 1999).

Innovative approaches: It is often mentioned that government approaches tend to follow a more uniform approach than the often innovative or more diverse approaches of CSOs, many of which work in difficult environments and with fewer resources (Middleton-Lee 2007). As mentioned by DFID (2004, 2006), CSOs play an important role, particularly in fragile states, by delivering services to poor people and developing innovative approaches to reducing HIV infection and socioeconomic marginalization (Alonso and Brugha 2006). The work done in India by the government and its development partners, including Ahavan, is an example of such an approach. By following a business model, Avahan was able to deliver an effective set of prevention and treatment services in six high-prevalence states with a combined population of 300 million.[1]

Populations reached by CSOs. Kelly et al.'s (2006) study of HIV prevention in 75 countries provides some indication of the population served by CSOs in four regions of the world (table 2.1). The general population was the main focus of most CSO-run HIV prevention programs, followed by youth programs. Injecting drug users (IDUs) were an important group for 56 percent of the CSOs working in Eastern Europe and Central Asia. With the exception of Latin America, prevention activities with MSM were uncommon, and few organizations had programs for sex workers or prisoners.

Table 2.1 Population Groups Reached by CSOs in Four Regions

Population reached	Africa (n = 27)	Central & Eastern Europe & Central Asia (n = 15)	Latin America (n = 15)	Caribbean (n = 48)
Youth	59% (16)	44% (11)	28% (4)	50% (4)
General population	67% (18)	32% (8)	60% (9)	63% (5)
Men who have sex with men	0	8% (2)	33% (5)	0
Injecting drug users	0	56% (14)	13%(2)	0
Sex workers	15% (4)	20% (5)	7% (1)	0
Prisoners	4% (4)	12% (3)	0	0
High risk heterosexuals	22% (7)	4% (1)	7% (1)	0
PWLHA	19% (5)	24% (6)	7% (1)	50% (4)

Source: Kelly et al. 2006.
Note: While the differences in population groups reached by CSOs in these four regions of the world might have reflected epidemiological differences, the low percentage or lack of CSOs working with certain high risk groups was also due to a number of legal and institutional barriers as well as lack of funding (UNAIDS 2008).

Institutional Design of the Community Response

Responses to the HIV epidemic have greatly evolved since the 1990s. In the early years, the responses were mainly run by ministries of health and were medically oriented. However, as the HIV epidemic continued to spread throughout the world, a broad consensus emerged that the HIV and AIDS response needed to be scaled up dramatically, especially by relying on CSOs. These organizations were viewed as offering a way to overcome government's limited capacity for rapidly increasing the delivery of services. However, implementation of this approach encountered a number of trade-offs which are at the core of many of the differences observed in how the four major donors design their funding channels. These are discussed in more detail below.

The World Bank MAP for Africa was the first to offer African countries substantial, long-term funding to support HIV programs at a national scale (World Bank 1999). At that time, there was a concern that national institutions and capacities for addressing the HIV epidemic needed to be strengthened or created. This process was viewed as essential for ensuring national ownership and sustainability of the programs over the long-term. In the countries where this program was implemented, the financial support tended to be provided to implementing entities (for example, ministries, local governments, and CSOs) rather than for specific kinds of interventions (for example, prevention or treatment). This approach had three important consequences. First, MAP projects directly earmarked a significant share of funding to CSOs and local governments that supported the community response. Second, MAP projects allocated another share of funding to various government ministries to support a multi-sectoral approach. Third, in some countries there was a specific fund allocated to CSOs rather than civil society in general (for example, Zambia and Uganda). These funds proved extremely successful in mobilizing a genuine community response and getting fund to these communities.[2] It is estimated that, during the 2003–06 period, over 66,000 CSOs and 234 line ministries received funding across Africa to respond to the HIV epidemic (Görgens-Albino *et al.* 2007).

High priority was given to institutional strengthening (33 percent of MAP funding) and community response—about 39 percent of MAP funding was focused on providing funding to small, national NGOs often operating at the community level) (Görgens-Albino *et al.* 2007). This approach proved successful in providing technical assistance to local governments—often the only source of international aid available for that purpose—and in providing small grants to a large number of small NGOs and CBOs. There was a drawback, however. Although funds were rapidly disbursed to national governments, sub-recipients often experienced difficulties in accessing funding whenever they did not have the needed capacity for meeting the reporting and accounting requirements. HIV and AIDS projects were also developed in other regions, either as stand-alone projects or as a component of other projects (for example, health, education, and transport).

The U.S. PEPFAR was designed as an emergency response to the HIV epidemic. This reflected a general agreement that the epidemic was exceptional and required an emergency response (Piot 2006). Consistent with this view, the program emphasized achieving specific targets in the 15 countries most affected by the epidemic, and within a relatively short period of five years. The program was designed to meet specific guidelines concerning the allocation of funds across programs, as well as the U.S. Government's financial and reporting requirements.

These priorities and constraints meant employing international CSOs with proven experience in managing development projects. This option was attractive as (1) it carried with it the likelihood of quickly scaling-up HIV and AIDS services and (2) it made it possible to fund substantial increases in the national AIDS responses while meeting fiduciary and accounting requirements of the donor agencies. Its main risks were that international CSOs might not accurately represent the real needs of communities to whom they were to provide services and few funds would actually trickle down to national NGOs, and especially CBOs.

In recent years, however, the number and composition of recipients has changed. The total number of PEPFAR partner organizations expanded from roughly 1,600 in fiscal 2004 to almost 2,700 in fiscal 2008, with 2,300 being national organizations. This trend is in line with the PEPFAR's objective to build national capacity.

PEPFAR's design has made it possible for the program to become the largest source of funding worldwide and has resulted in substantial achievements, especially in terms of access to treatment. Other objectives that have recently gained attention include better integrating the HIV and AIDS response, building national systems, and ensuring the sustainability of the AIDS response over the long term. As a result of these foci, the AIDS response is now becoming part of a broader health strategy.

The creation of the **Global Fund to Fight AIDS, Tuberculosis and Malaria (Global Fund)** was guided by the two principles of country ownership and performance-based funding.[3] These principles meant that countries themselves would develop proposals and selected recipients would implement them. This design led to the creation of the Country Coordinating Mechanism (CCM), which involves various stakeholders from civil society but with government representatives typically playing a prominent role. The CCM is responsible for submitting applications to the Global Fund and it nominates the Principal Recipients (PRs) that will manage the grant. Funds are disbursed by the Global Fund to the PRs who are responsible for choosing sub-recipients and overseeing the implementation of the proposals. This design gives a strong role to country ownership and implementation. It also allowed for rapid disbursement of funds to PRs, but there were still implementation problems at the level of the sub-recipients. Bottlenecks were encountered too, when these recipients lacked capacity to implement programs on a large scale and insufficient attention was given to fiduciary controls (a constraint that is now being addressed).

The UK DFID followed an approach that combined elements of two different models. At the global level, an institutional channel was created to provide funding to a relatively small number of large CSOs (that is, those with Partnership Programme Agreements). The goal was to achieve quick implementation of specific programs. And, at the country level, various funding channels were established to provide funding to national CSOs to pursue different objectives, such as reduction of stigma and gender discrimination. This approach allowed DFID's HIV and AIDS response to increase rapidly over a short period of time and to meet its funding target. However, DFID's focus on a number of longer-term, more qualitative objectives also exposed its HIV and AIDS response to criticism from the UK Parliament, which noted that implementation was not sufficiently monitored by quantifiable indicators. This criticism is not specific to DFID's strategy, but applies more generally to strategies that are aimed at generating changes (such as capacity building) over the longer term and are, thus, more difficult to measure.

Flow of Funds from Donors

The increased availability of funding has generated a number of paradoxes. At the country level, large sums of money have been allocated by donors to international NGOs and a few national NGOs for implementing projects, which often represented the priorities of donors. This led governments to complain that too much money is being spent on civil society. Yet at the community level, the opposite voice is heard, namely that CBOs, which are closer to local communities and likely to be more effective, receive too little money (Foster 2005). This situation explains the often heard view that money is being wasted on organizations that do not sufficiently contribute to the national AIDS response, while those that should be funded do not receive sufficient technical and financial support to have a significant impact.

Under one interpretation, insufficient funding at the community level could reflect insufficient funding at the global level. Providing more funding globally would then solve this problem. Under an alternative explanation, various bottlenecks are the prime reason that available funding does not reach certain local communities. In this latter case, the remedy is to improve the flow of funds but not to increase funding at the national level. To bring more clarity to the issue, this report analyzes funding flows and focuses on the following four questions:

1. What is the magnitude of the resource flows? Are the flows as small as suggested by some observers of the community response?
2. How are countries managing the inflow of resources for the community response?
3. How deep is the flow of resources, that is, do they reach CBOs?
4. Does the allocation of funding match the needs of local communities?

The available information and data sources that are summarized in table 2.2 provide a rough idea of the amount of funding that the four largest HIV and AIDS donors have made available to national CSOs as well as to international CSOs with national programs. Due to various limitations, the existing donor databases do not provide readily available information on the amounts disbursed to national CSOs, nor do they make it possible to trace the flow of funds from the national level to lower levels. To overcome these limitations various proxies were used to estimate the funding available for the community response.

Table 2.2 Summary of Donors' Funding of Civil Society Organizations

Donor	Proxy for the funding of community responses to AIDS	Period	Available funding for national AIDS responses (per year in US$)	Average per year for CSOs (US$)
World Bank	Share of CSO funding in MAP projects applied to all Bank projects for HIV&AIDS	June 2003–December 2010	$262 million	$100 million (indirect funding)
Global Fund	Expenditures by CSOs	2002–10	$910 million	$300 million (direct and indirect funding)
PEPFAR (USA)	Estimated funding for nonclinical activities reaching national CSOs	June 2003–December 2010	$2.1 billion	$230 million (mostly direct funding)
DFID (UK)	Estimated funds to CSO first-line recipients with AIDS as a major project or significant priority	2004/05–2008/09: (5 years)	$590 million	$60 million (mostly direct funding)
Total		Average in 2004–2009	$3.8 billion	At least 690 million

Source: World Bank and Global Fund database, and HIV/AIDS Alliance for DFID and PEPFAR data.

Overall, it is estimated that the four major donors provided at least US$690 million per year on average from 2004 to 2009 to national CSOs. In the case of World Bank and Global Fund, the estimates include the amounts "directly" received from donors and those that are given to national governments, which in turn transmit them to smaller NGOs. For the other donors, only the funding made available directly to CSOs could be estimated from the available information. As a result, the estimated funding for civil society is likely to underestimate the financial resources received by its organizations. Results are as follows:

The U.S. President's Emergency Plan for AIDS Relief

- In total, about US$2.1 billion was disbursed annually for HIV and AIDS from June 2003 to December 2010. Most of the funds were managed by first-line recipients, which were large consulting firms, international and national NGOs, universities, and FBOs. The funds received by national CSOs were taken to represent the financial resources that could be available for the community response. Funding received by international CSOs was excluded on the ground that these funds are likely to be spent on activities (for example, international consultants) that are unlikely to represent the community response. In total, it was estimated that national CSOs received on average US$230 million per year during the 2004–09 period, or about 11 percent of PEPFAR assistance.

The Global Fund to Fight AIDS, Tuberculosis and Malaria

- The funds disbursed for HIV and AIDS amounted to US$7.3 billion funding from 2002 to 2010 (Global Fund 2011). On average, one-third of the total funding for HIV, tuberculosis, and malaria was spent by CSOs. Applying this percentage to funding for HIV and AIDS suggests that US$300 million per year on average was disbursed by CSOs.

World Bank

- Information on the funding of national CSOs was obtained from an internal survey of MAP projects, which showed that 39 percent of the World Bank's MAP funding had been allocated to funding the civil society response in Africa. Financial resources were also provided to other regions, especially Latin America and Asia. As these projects followed a similar structure and purpose, it was assumed that these CSOs received a similar percentage of the funds that were provided by the World Bank.
- Projects during the last decade gave a high priority to financing the community response. In India, for example, the World Bank channeled 60 percent of its funding for HIV to CSOs. In fiscal 2004–09 World Bank disbursements of funds for HIV and AIDS projects (including HIV and AIDS components of projects) amounted to US$1.6 billion.[4] About US$100 million per year was provided to national NGOs and CBOs, which accessed national funding schemes established by governments (such as pooled funding). In many cases, this funding was the only substantial donor support for community and grassroots initiatives.

UK DFID

- On average, CSOs received an estimated US$56 million per year for HIV and AIDS during the 2004–09 period, which amounted to about 10 percent of DFID's total assistance for HIV and AIDS.
- These amounts were estimated from a recently created DFID database of projects. CSO funding for HIV and AIDS was estimated from the funding received by CSOs that were first-line recipients with AIDS and whose project showed HIV and AIDS as a principal or significant component.

In aggregate, donor funding for the community response is likely to exceed US$690 million per year on average. As shown by table 2.2, the funding share going to national CSOs varies greatly across donors. However, it would be incorrect to draw inferences from these differences as the estimated finding is based on proxies that may underestimate the total funding that is available for the community response. In the case of the World Bank, for example, funds are first disbursed to governments, which, in turn, transmit them to CSOs. The Global Fund and DFID also use this system of "indirect" funding, and it may exist in the case of PEPFAR. However, due to data limitations, it was not possible to estimate its size for DFID and PEPFAR. As the estimated funding from DFID, and PEPFAR takes into account only the "direct" funding that reaches national CSOs, it would be misleading to compare the allocation of donor funds.

Other Funding Flows

In addition to the financial aid provided by governments, there are other sources of funding. These include international NGOs that may be working with communities and funding flows coming from individuals, foundations, and charities in high income countries that are directed to funding specific activities in HIV affected countries. The available data suggest that in aggregate these funds amount to about US$600 million per year (UNAIDS 2010) with most of the funding coming from the United States. They are used to finance research and international organizations such as GAVI (Global Alliance for Vaccines and Immunisation), international NGOs, or specific programs in countries such as Brazil, China, India, Mexico, the Russian Federation, and South Africa. While in aggregate the flows reaching local communities in the countries affected by HIV and AIDS may be small, these funding streams are important for small NGOs and CBOs, as shown by country studies (appendix B).

Country Funding Profiles

Another way to get a sense of the magnitude of donor funding granted to CSOs, as well as to understand how this funding is used, is to look at several country case studies. The four countries reviewed in this study—Kenya, Nigeria, Peru, and India—present contrasting situations in terms of CSO involvement and funding.

India: There is a long tradition of CSOs operating at various levels in India, and CSOs are at the core of India's AIDS response. Under the NACP III, targeted interventions have expanded substantially. These are implemented by NGOs, and increasingly by CBOs, in partnership with government and they provide services to marginalized and hard-to-reach groups. Currently there are 1,609 targeted interventions covering 1.1 million high-risk groups that are implemented by 2,200 small NGOs/CBOs (India 2011). In total, the funding reaching CSOs amounts to at least 31 percent of the total resources for HIV and AIDS.

Several funding schemes reach small NGOs/CBOs in important ways. On the one hand, there is a relatively small group of large Indian and international CSOs that are receiving funding directly from donor agencies. Several of these CSOs act as intermediaries and provide sub-grants to grassroots organizations. On the other hand, there is a national funding mechanism (pool of funds established by the World Bank, DFID, and the government) that funds performance-based contracts of small NGOs and CBOs. Donors are also encouraged to fund technical support units at national and state levels, with the objective of increasing the management capacity of small NGOs and CBOs.

Despite a common perception that international donors are the lead funders for CSOs, the government probably supports the largest number of AIDS organizations, especially smaller NGOs and CBOs at district and state levels. Through these various channels, implementation on the ground is almost entirely carried out by organizations that are community-based or have links to local communities.

NGOs'/CBOs' activities are guided by a set of standardized interventions that have been defined by NACP III. These objectives are supported by the World Bank HIV and AIDS project. Funding is provided against a set of standardized interventions and is renewed depending on whether the agreed-upon objectives have been met.

Kenya: The government has a long history of supporting CSOs. Financial support for CSOs has been relatively substantial (US$86 million in 2007/08) amounting to 24 percent of the national spending on HIV and AIDS (Kenya 2009). Most of the donor funds for the community response were received by a few large NGOs at the national level with only a small fraction trickling down to CBOs at lower levels (2 percent of national spending). Data from the Evaluation of the Community Response to HIV and AIDS in Kenya indicate that CBOs' budgets are small: US$15,000 on average (and US$10,800 if one large CBO is excluded from the sample) in the communities that were surveyed in Western Kenya (World Bank 2011a).

However, this situation is changing as national funding mechanisms put in place by government and its development partners have helped channel funding to CBOs and helped increase the total funding received by the civil society. An important contributor was the World Bank first MAP project in Kenya (KADREP)[5] which allocated US$30 million out of a total US$50 million to the

Main Results

community response. Under this project over 6,000 community initiatives were funded, largely through small CBOs.

Further impetus to the community response is provided by Kenya's new National AIDS Strategic Plan (KNASP III 2009/10–2012/13). KNASP III gives much greater importance to the community response, which is now one of the key pillars of the national response. This policy is supported by the 2009 World Bank Total War on AIDS (TOWA) Project. Some 14 priority interventions were identified and provided the basis for issuing calls for proposals. So far, promising results have been achieved. As of August 2010, 2,225 project sub-implementers had been contracted and 4.5 million Kenyans had been reached in all the provinces. On average, CSOs (project sub-implementers) received about US$1,900 per year.[6] This funding served to fill critical gaps at the community level.

Results from the evaluation of the community response to HIV and AIDS (World Bank 2011a) showed that CBO activities complemented the national response. The surveyed CBOs spent proportionately fewer funds on treatment and care (15 percent compared to 55 percent for the national response) and more on impact mitigation (29 percent compared to 8 percent for the national response).

The Evaluation also revealed that communities with a stronger CBO involvement showed better knowledge of HIV prevention than those with a weaker involvement,[7] including having one partner infected (9 times more likely), using condoms (15 times more likely) and drugs to prevent mother-to-child transmission (4 times better knowledge) (figure 2.2).

A long-standing challenge is that small NGOs and CBOs have limited access to direct international funding as they are generally not in a position to meet

Figure 2.2 Strength of CBO Engagement and HIV Knowledge in Kenya

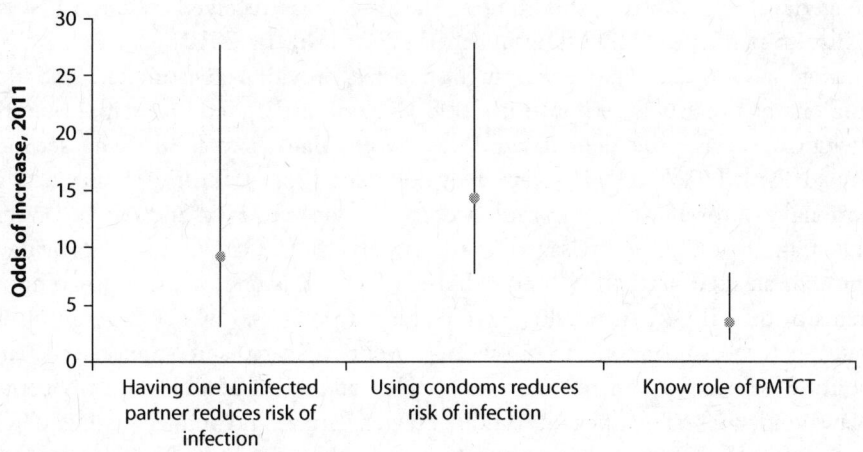

Source: World Bank 2011a.
Note: Dots = Odds ratio, Line = Confidence interval, PMTCT = Prevention of mother to child transmission.

specific donor requirements, such as monitoring and fiduciary controls. However, results from the evaluation of the community response in Kenya show that they have been able to access various funding channels, including direct donor funding. A majority of these funds were provided through national funding channels, namely the ministry of health (24 percent), local government (19 percent), foundations and charities (9 percent), and funds generated by the CBOs themselves (3 percent). Perhaps surprisingly, CBOs were able to directly access donor funding from multilateral and bilateral sources (45 percent of resources), indicating how much CBOs' situation had changed from earlier assessments, which concluded that few donor funds reached CBOs (Foster 2005).

Paradoxically, while donor funding increases CBOs resources, it also creates the risk that CBOs may be forced to stop operating if external funding decreases abruptly. In Kenya's case, this risk is mitigated by the nature of these CBOs. The CBOs that were surveyed in the Nyanza and Western Provinces were found to operate with few or no permanent staff but a large number of volunteers (21 per CBO on average). While some received compensation, others did not. The estimated value of unpaid volunteers' time represented over 40 percent of CBOs' financial resources.[8] Volunteers represent an important resource which is likely to continue to exist as they work for an organization that serves their communities. These findings showed that CBOs leveraged government and international funding and, in the process, increased the resources of the national AIDS response.

Nigeria: In parallel with a democratization process that started in 1999, Nigeria began working toward a national response to HIV and AIDS at all levels of government and society. The role of CSOs in the AIDS response increased with improvements in the political environment. A great diversity of CSOs is now involved in care from informal self-help organizations to consortium representing people living with HIV and AIDS (PLWHA). On aggregate, CSOs have become the main providers of HIV and AIDS services. They spent US$200 million in 2008, delivering 53 percent of the country's HIV and AIDS services (Nigeria 2010). Most of this funding, however, was received by large CSOs. Only 1.5 percent of AIDS flows reached CBOs (Nigeria 2010).

Nigeria's international development partners provided an estimated US$395 million for the AIDS response in 2008 (Nigeria 2010). The principal donors include PEPFAR, the Global Fund, the World Bank, and DFID. The second World Bank HIV/AIDS Program Development Project (HPDP2) supports a national, comprehensive, and multisectoral response to HIV and AIDS. Under this framework, it is envisaged that support to CSOs would be provided through an HIV and AIDS fund (HAF). The HAF is one of the core components of the HPDP2. It would provide grants to NGOs, FBOs, CBOs, and private sector organizations to provide prevention, care, and support; sustain political will; and mobilize resources for HIV and AIDS at all levels in Nigeria. New guidelines are aimed at funding fewer, larger, and longer lasting CSO projects with better performance management and results-based financing. Successful projects would receive extended or scaled-up financing. As there is a

Main Results

risk that CSOs with limited capacity to develop and manage projects would not qualify for funding, the project would fund "service support organizations" to deliver technical capacity building.

At the national level, donors and external sources funded most of Nigeria's AIDS response (92 percent). At the community level, the funding structure is different. Findings from the evaluation of the community response to HIV and AIDS in Nigeria indicated that CBOs mobilized on average US$17,000 per year (World Bank 2011b). Direct funding from bilateral and multilateral sources represented 33 percent of the resources that CBOs received. Funds from foundations, charities, and other national and international NGOs accounted for 48 percent. An additional 10 percent came from the funding channel created by the national government and 9 percent from CBOs' members and income-generating activities. This funding structure highlighted the diversity of funding sources that the Nigerian CBOs are able to mobilize.

Data from the Evaluation of the Community Response to HIV and AIDS illustrate the positive impact played by CBOs, especially in rural areas where access to services is likely to be more difficult than in urban areas. On average, adding one more CBO per 100,000 residents in rural areas was associated with a more than twofold increase in the likelihood that a respondent would report using prevention services, a 64 percent increase in the likelihood that a community resident would use treatment services, and a 32 percent likelihood that he or she received care and support (World Bank 2011b) (figure 2.3).

This data also provided information on the funding and allocation of expenditures for 41 surveyed CBOs. As in Kenya, their budget was small (US$10,900 on average). CBOs were found to spend the most on prevention (25 percent of

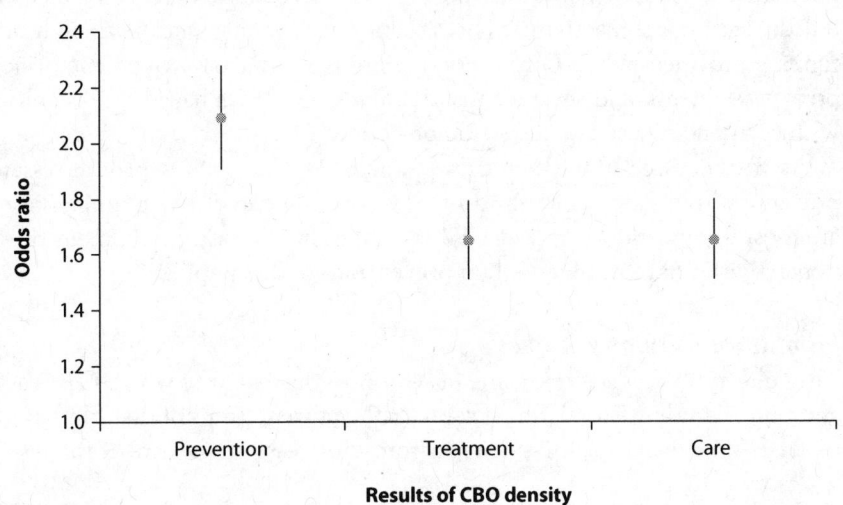

Figure 2.3 CBO Density and Service Use in Rural Areas in Nigeria

Source: World Bank 2011b.
Note: Dots = Odds ratio, Line = confidence interval.

expenditures) and mitigation of socioeconomic impact (23 percent), followed by AIDS treatment and care services (22 percent). The rest of the expenditures were allocated to capacity building (12 percent) and program management (18 percent). This pattern differed substantially from the national AIDS response, which allocated 63 percent of its funding to treatment and care (Nigeria 2010).

As was the case in Kenya, CBOs relied on volunteers for most of their work. On average, CBOs employed 58 volunteers, some of whom received compensation. Using the compensation paid to these volunteers to estimate the value of the work provided by unpaid volunteers indicated that volunteers represented a substantial resource equal to 48 percent of the CBOs' financial resources. This suggests that CBOs increase the total resources available to the national AIDS response.

Peru: The involvement of CSOs in the HIV and AIDS response is relatively recent in Peru. On average, the funds that donors made available to CSOs amounted to US$11 million per year (33 percent) of the total funding in 2006–08.[9] As in Kenya, the existing data show that a limited number of CSOs received most of the international funding (almost 70 percent of funding went to five CSOs). In addition, intermediary support of smaller NGOs was less common than in other countries.

The Global Fund was the largest funding source for CSOs, representing almost 35 percent of revenue for all of civil society's externally funded projects. Four health research centers were the next most important source of funds (at 44 percent). These centers were all based in the United States and, presumably, were channeling centrally awarded U.S. Government funding to CSOs in Peru.

Historically, there is not a long tradition of Peruvian CSOs acting as intermediary organizations for HIV/AIDS funding. While national CSOs worked with grassroots groups, the responsibility for managing financial resources and supplier contracts was kept with national CSOs. The contracted CBOs only carried out the agreed-upon activities. This situation is now changing. As a result of the funding provided by the Global Fund, more CSOs have now become principal project recipients, and several consortia involving CSOs have been established, with each one focused on a specific objective.

As in the three other countries studied, Peruvian CSOs play an essential prevention role. About one-third of CSO projects target key populations who are most significantly at risk of HIV infection. In contrast, government prevention activities have not focused on prevention for key populations.

Insights from Country Studies

The country studies provide some insights into the extent to which CSOs access and utilize funding and highlight some of the current limits of that funding. Two of the main conclusions that emerge from these case studies are as follows:

- **Funding of CSOs account for a relatively large share of total AIDS flows**: 31 percent in India, 24 percent in Kenya, 33 percent in Peru and 51 percent in Nigeria.

Main Results

Figure 2.4   AIDS Resources Received by CSOs and CBOs

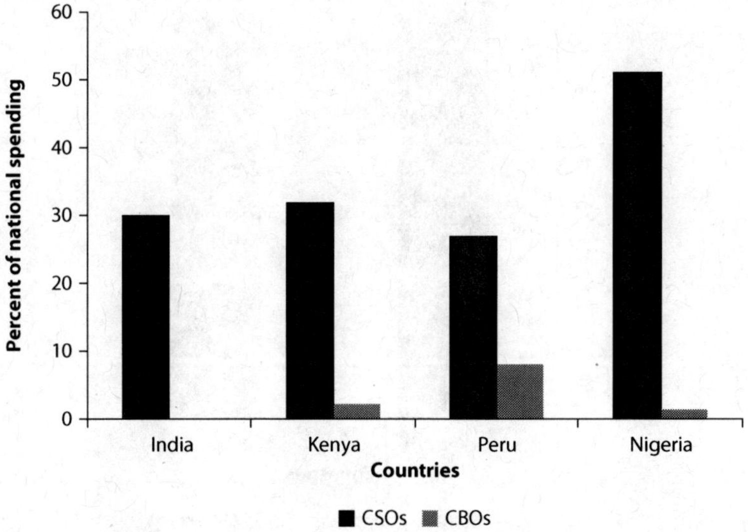

[Bar chart showing percent of national spending by country for CSOs and CBOs:
- India: CSOs ~30%, CBOs 0
- Kenya: CSOs ~32%, CBOs ~2%
- Peru: CSOs ~27%, CBOs ~8%
- Nigeria: CSOs ~51%, CBOs ~1.5%]

Sources: India: estimate based on available data on donor funding in 2010; Kenya: 2008 data from the 2009 National Spending Assessment; Nigeria: 2008 data from the 2010 National Spending Assessment; Peru: 2006–08 data from the records of APCI (Peruvian Agency of International Cooperation).

- **Large CSOs receive the largest share:** Examples from three country studies (Kenya, Nigeria, and Peru) show substantial differences between large CSOs and small CBOs. CBOs received a small share of international funding: 1.5 percent in Nigeria, 2 percent in Kenya, 8 percent or less in Peru (figure 2.4). This situation largely reflects the difficulties experienced by small NGOs and CBOs in accessing such funding due to their limited capacity to meet donors' financial reporting and monitoring requirements. In addition, CBOs are often not registered, which means they lack legal status and they may not have the government endorsement to receive funding from external sources. However, when there is strong government commitment, small NGOs/CBOs as in India can access funding.
- **CBOs mobilize other financial resources**. Information from surveyed CBOs in Kenya and Nigeria show that funding provided by national funding channels set up by governments, aid from foundations and charities as well as CBOs' own fund raising have become more important than the international funding reaching CBOs directly (figure 2.5). A similar conclusion is provided by the International HIV/AIDS Alliance survey of small NGOs, which showed that national funding mechanisms, foundations and charities and private fund raising accounted for 47 percent of NGOs' income (table 2.4).
- **CBOs and NGOs also mobilize a large number of paid and unpaid volunteers.** In Kenya the surveyed CBOs "employed" 21 volunteers per CBO on average. In Nigeria the corresponding number was 51 volunteers and in Zimbabwe the surveyed 196 NGOs employed 196 volunteers on average.

Figure 2.5 Source of CBO Funding in Kenya and Nigeria (2011)

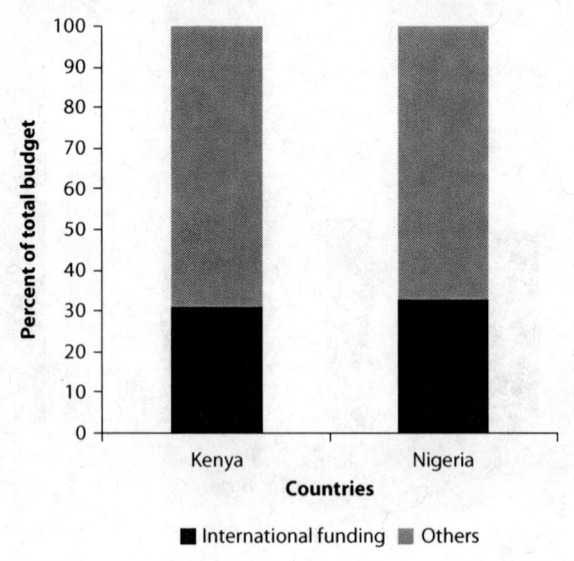

Sources: World Bank 2011a, 2011b.

Table 2.3 Value of Unpaid Volunteers as a percent of CBOs/NGOs' Budget

	Kenya	Nigeria	Zimbabwe
Number of volunteers per CBOs/NGOs	21	58	196
Value of unpaid volunteers' free labor as % of CBOs/NGOs' budget	40%	48%	69%

Sources: World Bank 2011a, 2011b, 2011c.

A large number of these volunteer did not receive any monetary compensation. Yet, the value of the free volunteer labor is substantial: it represents an estimated 40 percent of CBOs financial resources in Kenya, 38 percent in Nigeria and 69 percent in Zimbabwe (table 2.3), indicating that small NGOs and CBOs increase the total resources of national AIDS response.
- Information from the International HIV/AIDS survey also confirmed the importance of volunteers. Half or more of the CSOs' workforces consisted of volunteers and a third to a half were volunteers. Overall, only 11 percent of the workforce was not volunteers (figure 2.6).
- **Small NGOs/CBOs represent a largely underutilized source of service provision.** Small organizations can play a substantial role in implementing the AIDS response, such as in India, where CBOs are viewed as essential partners for delivering specific interventions at the community level. In other countries, the expansion of CBOs' role has been hampered by the lack of a road map that would frame their intervention. As a result the activities of these CBOs have not always been consistent with the priorities of national AIDS responses.

Main Results

Figure 2.6 Proportion of Volunteers in CSOs' Workforce (2011)

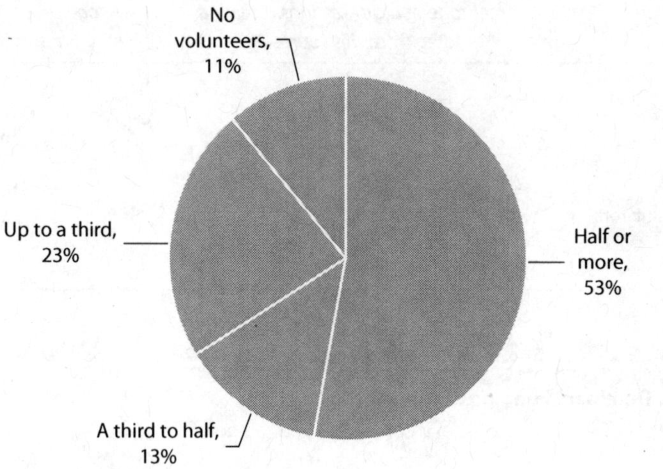

- No volunteers, 11%
- Up to a third, 23%
- A third to half, 13%
- Half or more, 53%

Source: International HIV/AIDS Alliance survey 2010.

International HIV/AIDS Alliance Survey of CSOs

The CSOs that responded to a survey conducted by the International HIV/AIDS Alliance in 2010 represented mainly small to medium-size organizations—two-thirds had less than 20 staff—and they relied greatly on volunteers. Some of the CSOs work at the national level, but, more often, at the subnational and local levels (see appendix C for more details). Given the diverse nature of CSOs, the sample is not representative of all CSOs involved in the AIDS response. For instance, there were a few large, international NGOs among the respondents, but most of the surveyed CSOs were small organizations (71 percent were NGOs/CBOs). Others were FBOs, associations of people living with HIV (PLWH), and advocacy organizations. A large proportion came from developing countries (89 percent), with the geographical spread covering all regions.

CSOs' principal funding sources included the Global Fund (21 percent), own fund-raising (16 percent), national funding mechanisms (16 percent), bilateral and multilateral donors (16 percent), and foundations or charities (15 percent) (table 2.4). The three sources of funding that respondents cited most often were the organizations' own fund-raising, national funding mechanisms, and foundations or charities. The Global Fund was the fourth most often cited source of funding. Bilateral donors were also mentioned by about one-third of the CSOs. This relatively weak identification of bilateral aid could occur if such funding passed through intermediaries and the government, or if this funding did not reach small, local organizations working at the grassroots.

The proportion of income from any single source suggests a significant level of reliance on donor funding among the CSOs in the sample (figure 2.7). Donor governments and multilateral financial institutions, including the Global Fund,

Table 2.4 Frequency and Average Distribution of Annual Funding among CSOs (2010)

Most important annual income sources in past financial year	Percentage of organizations receiving funding from this source (%)	Average proportion of income from this source (%)
The Global Fund	38	21
Private fund-raising	55	16
National funding mechanisms	42	16
Foundations or charities	42	15
DFID, PEPFAR, World Bank	29	10
Other bilateral donors or multilateral Institutions	34	16
Others	35	6

Source: International HIV/AIDS Alliance Survey 2010.

Figure 2.7 Dominant Funding Sources for CSOs (2010)
percentage of CSOs with over 50% of income from one category

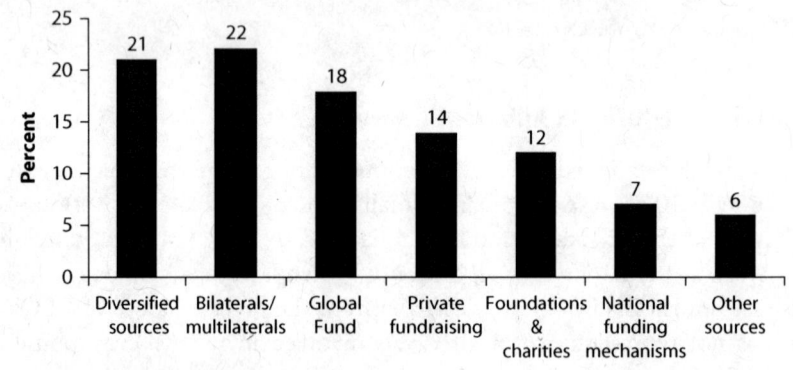

Category	Percent
Diversified sources	21
Bilaterals/multilaterals	22
Global Fund	18
Private fundraising	14
Foundations & charities	12
National funding mechanisms	7
Other sources	6

Source: International HIV/AIDS Alliance Survey 2010.

were a dominant source of funding for 40 percent of the CSOs.[10] This suggests that these CSOs are vulnerable to reductions in external aid from those sources. A further 12 percent of the CSOs cited name "foundations or charities" as a dominant funder. However, a third of organizations were not heavily reliant on income from single donor sources: 21 percent had no single source providing more than half of annual income and an additional 14 percent relied mostly on private fund-raising.

What Did the CSOs Do with Their Funding?

- *They deliver prevention activities.* These are the largest area of CSO annual expenditures, accounting for 42 percent of spending on average (figure 2.8). Within this total, 44 percent was spent on activities reaching high risk groups, people living with HIV, and their partners. Twenty percent went for awareness raising and prevention activities for the general population.
- *They provide care and support* to PLWHA, orphans and vulnerable children (OVC), and other adult members (19 percent of expenditures) as well as

Main Results

Figure 2.8 Allocation of Expenditures by CSOs

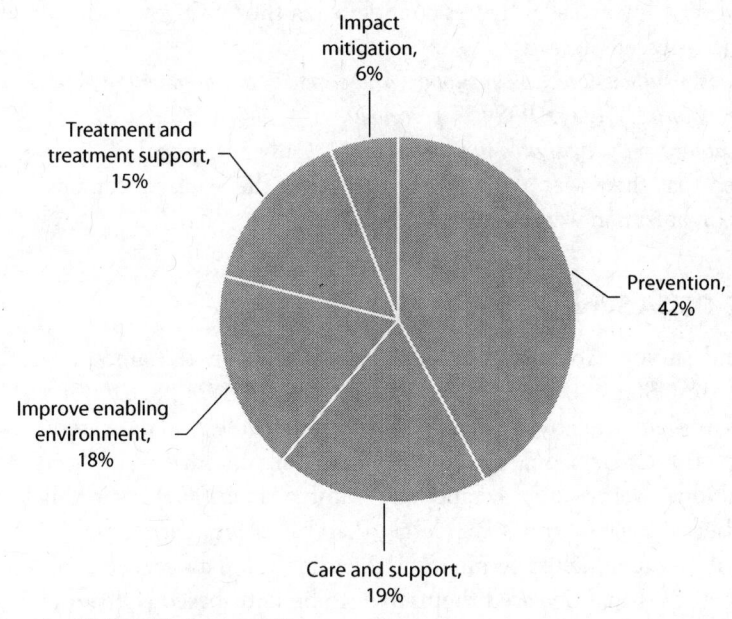

- Impact mitigation, 6%
- Treatment and treatment support, 15%
- Prevention, 42%
- Care and support, 19%
- Improve enabling environment, 18%

Source: International HIV/AIDS Alliance survey 2010.

activities aimed at **improving the enabling environment** (18 percent of expenditures).
- *They provide treatment activities that consist mainly of support for PLWHA* (15 percent of expenditures), for example, to help them gain access to clinical services or support to understand treatment adherence rather than actual drug procurement or provision.
- Finally, *they provide impact mitigation*, which accounted, on average, for only 6 percent of annual expenditures.

What Are the Main CSOs' Concerns?

The survey also asked for opinions on a number of specific issues. The answers relied on the views of participating individuals, but they provided at least some insight into the thinking among a subset of CSOs. CSOs respondents indicated the following:

- *More funding is needed.* Some 74 percent of respondents thought that more funding needs to be allocated to activities that reach vulnerable and most-at-risk populations.
- *The economic crisis felt by the United States and EU countries is affecting them.* Pressure on their budget was reported by 73 percent of respondents.
- *They were fairly confident in the quality of community action in their countries* (64 percent agreed). However, 51 percent were somewhat less confident about its comprehensiveness.

- *They expressed confidence in the collaboration among CSOs* (59 percent agreed). However, they had slightly less confidence in the CSO-government collaboration (51 percent agreed).
- *There is insufficient technical support and capacity development available to CSOs working on HIV and AIDS (57 percent).*
- *The quality of the available funding was low.* Only 51 percent of the respondents agreed that there was a good match between the available funding and what their organization wanted them to do.

CADRE-OSISA Survey

A second survey provides additional information on the amount of funding available to CSOs and how these organizations are using that funding. The survey was implemented by CADRE-OSISA, which collected data among approximately 400 CSOs from six southern African countries (Lesotho, Malawi, Mozambique, Namibia, Swaziland, and Zambia) in 2006/07 (Birdsall and Kelly 2007). Because the sample size is larger than the survey carried out by the HIV/AIDS International Alliance mentioned earlier, the data can be analyzed separately for CSOs that declared themselves to be faith-based (Olivier and Wodon 2011). Such an analysis helps understand how important are FBOs and whether they have different characteristics from other secular CSOs, as some have suggested. About one-third of the CSOs in the survey declared themselves to be faith-based (FB-CSOs). The other two-thirds that did not, will be considered as secular (S-CSOs).

The analysis of the survey suggests that there were a few differences between the types of CSOs (Olivier and Wodon 2011). The proportion of FB-CSOs that had branches or programs in other countries (18 percent) was higher than for S-CSOs (10 percent), and the proportion of FB-CSOs that were part of an HIV and AIDS association or coordinating network/body (90 percent) was also slightly higher than for S-CSOs (83 percent). Also, 72 percent of FB-CSOs conducted activities not related to HIV and AIDS, versus 64 percent of S-CSOs.

In the sample, FB-CSOs tended to be slightly more international, connected to other organizations working on HIV and AIDS, and more active in other areas than was the case for S-CSOs. Another difference was that, as expected, S-CSOs tended to have a higher ratio of paid staff (full-time or part-time) to volunteers than was the case for FB-CSOs. The data also suggested that FB-CSOs were somewhat more active in treatment, care, and support, as well as in impact mitigation and management than was the case for S-CSOs. By contrast, S-CSOs were slightly more active in prevention, as well as in policy, advocacy, and research. But overall, differences in activity profiles tended to be small.

The survey provided data on expenditure and funding for the period 2001–05. It showed that average levels of spending on HIV and AIDS rose sharply over time, with the average level of spending among S-CSOs amounting to US$160,141 in 2005, versus US$150,613 for FB-CSOs. Expenditures for both groups were about three times lower in 2001. Three main observations can be made. First, the likelihood of funding had increased for all types of donors over time. Second, the largest increase in funding was for national, provincial, or district HIV and AIDS structures. Third, FB-CSOs tended to report slightly different funding sources than did S-CSOs, probably due, in part, to the former's support from religiously affiliated groups.

Information was also gathered on broader changes in the funding environment. There was clear recognition that the availability of funding had increased, which also meant an increase in the time allocated for fund-raising. The number of grant proposals submitted by each CSO was about six per year, with a success rate of about 30 percent. About one-third of the CSOs stated that they had started new programs mainly because funding was offered for those activities. But 60 percent of CSOs also stated that they had cut back on some areas of activity because of lack of funding. Uncertainty about the availability of funding for programs in the following year suggested a high level of vulnerability among both FB-CSOs and S-CSOs to any decrease in HIV and AIDS funding.

Conclusion

This review attempted to triangulate existing and new information to answer questions about funding flows to the community AIDS response. Its results help answer the questions that motivated this study, namely, how large is the donor's funding of the community response; how do the funds reach CSOs; what are the CSOs' main funding sources; and what are these funds used for?

Donor funding is relatively substantial. In total, the four donors most actively involved in the AIDS response have provided US$690 million a year for civil society AIDS activities, with the actual amount likely to be higher if the indirect funding to CSOs through governments and other grantees by DFID and PEFAR was taken into account.

Donor funding has increased substantially. The CADRE-OSISA survey, for example, suggests that funding and program expenditures for CSOs in six countries in southern Africa increased threefold between 2001 and 2005. Further increases took place in recent years, especially due to increased funding by the Global Fund.

Donor Funding Has Facilitated the Expansion of CSOs through Various Channels

- Provision of direct funding by donors stimulated the expansion of large international or national CSOs. This was viewed as a desirable step for rapidly scaling up the AIDS response in a manner that would generate tangible results that could be monitored.

- At the country level, the channeling of donor assistance through national funding mechanisms has resulted in the creation or expansion of small and medium-sized NGOs that would not otherwise have been able to access such funding. In Kenya, Nigeria, and India, World Bank HIV and AIDS projects, include DFID support, disbursed funds through government channels reaching small CBOs. Global Fund policies that CBOs be included in the rounds also helped increase CBOs' access to donor funding.
- The rapid expansion in the number of CSOs has created a fragmented implementation of projects. This has led to the establishment of various coordination mechanisms, but they have largely remained specific to each funding flows established by donors.

Large CSOs are the main conduit for international aid. Most of donors' international aid is received by a few large CSOs. A key factor has been their ability to disburse funds quickly and meet donors' requirements in terms of financial reporting, monitoring of activities, and fiduciary controls. To that extent, they represent a substitute rather than a complement to government funding.

Small NGO/CBO activities complement the national AIDS response. Each of the four country profiles and the survey results confirm that the civil society response has helped to meet crucial needs.

- In India, some large standardized interventions, such as targeted prevention, relied fully on locally based CBO implementers, which were viewed as the best way to reach the high-risk groups they served.
- In Kenya, while donor-funded and government AIDS spending was dominated by treatment and care, CBOs' funds were allocated mainly to prevention and impact mitigation.
- In Nigeria, the surveyed CBOs indicated that they allocated funds nearly equally across prevention, mitigation of socioeconomic impact, and treatment and care. In contrast, the national AIDS program was heavily focused on treatment and care (47 percent of resources), with smaller funding amounts allocated to prevention and even less allocated to the mitigation of the effects of the epidemic.
- In Peru, one-third of CSO projects targeted most-at-risk population groups, including transgender people, MSM, and sex workers—groups that governmental prevention activities would not have focused on.

However, small NGOs and CBOs suffer from weak capacity to meet the various requirements attached to funding flows as well as to implement projects that would complement government programs. These shortcomings limit the complementary role that NGOs and CBOs can play. Addressing these constraints would require much more technical assistance than is currently available.

The survey of CSOs conducted by the International HIV/AIDS Alliance showed a similar focus on key activities. However, the survey also revealed a relatively widespread dissatisfaction with the current community response. Critical components such as the focus of the community response, the coordination among CSOs and between CSOs and the government, the quality of funding, and the technical assistance available for capacity development were the focus of criticisms by 40–50 percent of the respondents, with a higher percentage (73 percent) mentioning that more funding should be allocated to prevention activities for high risk groups.

Strategic Policy Questions

There is little doubt that in the countries that were studied for this report, civil society as implementer of the national response has been fully embraced by the donor community. But this seems to have been done mainly as a way of enlarging the scope of the HIV and AIDS response rather than in response to the strengths and weaknesses of CSOs. The overall result has been an expansion of CSOs that is often taking place without a clear road map (with the exception of some countries such as India) that would indicate how their involvement should be aligned with National AIDS Strategies and coordinated with government programs. In some countries in Africa, the result has been growing tensions and frictions between civil society and HIV and AIDS authorities, especially in the countries with the highest HIV prevalence rate and the greatest funding flows. These tensions may become more explicit as funding for HIV and AIDS becomes scarcer.

The evidence provided by the recent evaluation of the community response helps strengthen the case that CBOs can play a role that complements effectively the national HIV and AIDS response. But there were also cases where no effects could be found. These results suggest that the efficiency of the community response could be improved.

In most discussions of the community response, increased effectiveness of the community response is often equated with a need for additional funding. By providing more money to where it is needed the most, only part of the problem faced by CBOs can be addressed. In most cases, and especially for CBOs, obtaining access to funding is only one step as the value of the funding provided to CBOs greatly depends on other kinds of support, in particular, technical training. One of the great assets of the surveyed CBOs is the large number of volunteers they relied upon. But their biggest constraint is the difficulty volunteers faced in obtaining adequate technical training. Without it, it is difficult to see how the efficiency of CBOs' interventions could improve.

Mechanisms that have been used to increase access to funding and technical assistance include the creation of umbrella organizations, the provision of training by larger NGOs to smaller ones, and government/donor support for technical assistance. So far, there are few incentives for small organizations to increase their effectiveness, but this situation is changing as donors are shifting their assistance toward performance-based contracting. Most likely, this will increase the incentives for CSOs to access technical assistance.

These trends, if pursued, will shift the functioning of some CSOs away from their traditional independence from government toward a much greater cooperation with government ministries. In this case, they could become implementers of services that they are better positioned to provide. In this new function, much greater importance will be attached to the effectiveness of resource allocation and the evaluation of the results obtained by CSOs' activities, including at the local level where many small NGOs work. To carry out these new functions, coordination of tasks between these NGOs and other entities will become much more important.

The implications of such a change are, however, mixed. While standardization of funding is probably needed for increasing the effectiveness of the community response, it may still be beneficial to maintain a mix of funding modalities. A fundamental characteristic of CSOs is their heterogeneity, which implies that only a differentiated system of funding can provide the flexibility and diversity of objectives that CSOs currently pursue. These conclusions suggest that a delicate balance needs to be maintained between harmonizing the institutional mechanisms for providing support to CSOs, including small NGOs and CBOs, and maintaining CSOs' access to direct funding from various sources.

Notes

1. The Avahan initiative is funded by the Bill & Melinda Foundation. See http://www.gatesfoundation.org/avahan/Documents/Avahan_FactSheet.pdf.
2. For more information, see http://www.aidsportal.org/repos/Uganda_CHAI.pdf.
3. See: History of the Global Fund. http://www.theglobal fund.org/en/whowearehistory.
4. In total, HIV and AIDS project commitments amounted to US$3.4 billion for the period 1989–2010.
5. Kenya HIV/AIDS Disaster Response.
6. The amount of funding is relatively small because its use is limited to specific items. For instance, it cannot be used for paying wages.
7. The involvement of CBOs was measured by the percentage of households which were aware of CBO activities in their community.
8. Volunteers who were compensated received on average US$0.3 per hour. This hourly wage was used to estimate the value of unpaid volunteers' time.
9. Records of Peruvian Agency of International Cooperation (APCI).
10. Dominant funders were deemed to be those providing more than half an organization's annual income.

References

Alonso, A., and R. Brugha. 2006. "Rehabilitating the Health System after Conflict in East Timor: A Shift from NGO to Government Leadership." *Health Policy and Planning* 21 (3): 206–16.

Birdsall, K., and K. Kelly. 2007. *Pioneers, Partners, Providers: The Dynamics of Civil Society and AIDS Funding in Southern Africa.* Johannesburg: Centre for AIDS Development, Research and Evaluation CADRE/Open Society Initiative for Southern Africa.

DANIDA (Danish International Development Agency). 2005. *Strategy for Denmark's Support to the International Fight against HIV/AIDS.* Copenhagen: DANIDA.

Delion, J. 2004. "Experience in Scaling Up Support to Local Response in Multi-Country Aids Programs (MAP) in Africa." Act Africa. Washington, DC: World Bank.

DFID (UK Department for International Development). 2004. "Taking Action: The UK's Strategy for Tackling HIV and AIDS in the Developing World." Strategy Paper, DFID, London.

———. 2006. "Civil Society and Development: How DFID Works in Partnership with Civil Society to Deliver Millennium Development Goals." Civil Society Team, DFIF, London; DFID.

Dongier, P., J. Van Domelen, E. Ostrom, A. Ryan, W. Wakeman, A. Bebbington, S. Alkire, T. Esmail, and M. Polski. 2001. "Community Driven Development." *World Bank, PRSP Sourcebook.* Vol. 1. Washington, DC: World Bank.

Drew, R., and K. Attawell. 2007. "Interim Evaluation of Taking Action: The UK Government's Strategy for Tackling HIV and AIDS in the Developing World—Final Report." DFID, London.

Foster, G. 2005. *Bottleneck and Drip-Feeds: Channelling Resources to Communities Responding to Orphans and Vulnerable Children in Southern Africa.* London: Save the Children.

Global Fund (Global Fund to Fight AIDS, Tuberculosis and Malaria). 2011. "Making a Difference: Global Fund Results Report 2011." The Global Fund, Geneva.

Görgens-Albino, M., N. Mohammad, D. Blankhart, and O. Odutolu. 2007. *The Africa Multi-country AIDS Program 2000–2006: Results of the World Bank's Response to a Development Crisis.* Washington, DC: World Bank.

Homedes, N., and A. Ugalde. 2006. "Improving Access to Pharmaceuticals in Brazil and Argentina." *Health Policy and Planning* 21 (2): 123–31.

International HIV/AIDS Alliance. 2007. *Supporting Civil Society Organisations to Reach Key Populations in the Latin American and Caribbean Region—A Look at HIV/AIDS Projects Financed by the World Bank.* Hove, UK: International HIV/AIDS Alliance.

ITPC (International Treatment Preparedness Coalition). 2008. "CCM Advocacy Report: Making Global Fund Country Coordination Mechanisms Work through Full Engagement of Civil Society." ITPC, Bangkok.

Kaiser (Henry J. Kaiser Family Foundation). 2012. *Financing the Response to AIDS in Low- and Middle-Income Countries: International Assistance from the G8, European Commission and Other Donor Governments in 2011.* Washington, DC. http://www.kff.org/hivaids/7347.cfm.

Kelly, J. A., A. M. Somlai, E. G. Benotsch, Y. A. Amirkhanian, M. I. Fernandez, L. Y. Stevenson, C. A. Sitzler, T. L. McAuliffe, K. D. Brown, and K. M. Opgenorth. 2006. "Programmes, Resources, and Needs of HIV-Prevention Nongovernmental Organizations (NGOs) in Africa, Central/Eastern Europe and Central Asia, Latin America and the Caribbean." *Aids Care—Psychological and Socio-Medical Aspects of AIDS/HIV* 18 (1): 12–21.

Kenya. 2009. "Kenya National AIDS Spending Assessment (NASA) Report for the Financial Years 2006/07 and 2007/08." Nairobi, Kenya: Kenya National AIDS Control Council.

Middleton-Lee, S. 2007. *Coordinating with Communities*. Toronto: ICASO, AfriCASO, International HIV/AIDS Alliance.

Nigeria. 2010. "National AIDS Spending Assessment (NASA) for the period 2007–2008", Abuja, Nigeria: National Agency for the Control of AIDS.

Noack, P., and M. Campioni. 2006. "Technical Consultation to the Global Partners Forum on Children Affected by HIV and AIDS: Universal Access to Prevention, Treatment and Care." London. February 7–8.

Olivier, J. and Q. Wodon. 2011. Layers of Evidence: Discourses and Typologies on Faith-Inspired Community Responses to HIV/AIDS in Africa, Mimeo. Washington, DC: World Bank.

Piot, P. 2006. "AIDS: From Crisis Management to Sustained Strategic Response." *The Lancet* 368: 526–30.

Sidaction, UNAIDS (Joint United Nations Programme on HIV/AIDS), and WHO (World Health Organization). 2005. "Expanding Access to HIV Treatment through Community-Based Organizations." UNAIDS Best Practice Collection, UNAIDS, Geneva.

UNAIDS (Joint United Nations Programme on HIV/AIDS). 2008. "Report on the Global Epidemic 2008." UNAIDS, Geneva.

———. 2010. *What Countries Need; Investments Needed for 2010 Targets*. Geneva: UNAIDS.

———. 2012. *Together We Will End AIDS*. Geneva: UNAIDS.

World Bank. 1999. *Intensifying Action against HIV/AIDS in Africa: Responding to a Development Crisis*. Washington, DC: World Bank.

———. 2003. "World Development Report 2004: Making Services Work for the Poor." World Bank and Oxford University Press, Washington, DC.

———. 2011a. Riehman, K., B. Manteuffel, B. Kakietek, J. Fruh, P. Kizito, L. Vane, R. Rodriguez-Garcia, R., Bonnel, N. N'Jie, K. Bigmore, and W. Ikua. *Effects of the Community Response to HIV and AIDS in Kenya*. Washington, DC: World Bank.

———. 2011b. Idoko J. O., J. Anenih, A. Akinrogunde, S. A. Gar, I. Jalingo, T. O. Ojogun, D. Fasiku, B. Ibrahim, S. M. O. Unogu, J. Kakietek, T. Gebreselassie, B. Manteuffel, A. Krivelyova, S. Bausche, J. Fruh, R. Rodriguez-Garcia, R. Bonnel, N. N'Jie, M. O'Dwyer, and F. A. Akala. *Effects of the Community Response to HIV and AIDS in Nigeria*. Washington, DC: World Bank.

———. 2011c. Gregson, S., C. Nyamukape, L. Sherr and C. Campbell. *Evaluation of the Community Responses to HIV and AIDS: Building Competent Communities: Evidence from Eastern Zimbabwe*. Washington, DC: World Bank.

APPENDIX A

Donor Funding Flows

This appendix focuses on the funding provided by the four largest AIDS donors (World Bank; the Global Fund to Fight AIDS, Tuberculosis and Malaria; the United States; and the United Kingdom). Together they account for over 80 percent of the assistance provided by G8 and other donors from the European Community (Kaiser 2010b).

The World Bank's HIV/AIDS Program

By the late 1990s, the World Bank recognized that a more comprehensive, multi-sectoral approach was needed to respond to what was perceived as not only an unprecedented health crisis, but also a development crisis. Hence, the World Bank developed a strategy that called for a new way to quickly provide resources, both to government and civil society sectors, within sound national HIV and AIDS frameworks. The Multi-Country HIV/AIDS Program for Africa (MAP), created in 2000, was a central part of the new strategy for Africa.

MAP Design

The overall objective of the MAP was to rapidly increase access to prevention, treatment, care and support, and mitigation programs. To achieve this, the MAP implemented a funding architecture that differed from previous Bank projects for HIV. First, it funded implementing entities (for example, ministries, local governments, and CSOs) rather than selected interventions. Second, in recognizing the role of social mobilization in building an effective HIV and AIDS response, the World Bank provided much more funding directly to communities and CSOs. In some countries, a specific fund was established for CSOs rather than civil society in general. And third, it funded a multi-sectoral response that involved all government ministries and agencies.

The MAP included three main channels for financial assistance:

- A component to disburse funds to civil society either by granting funds directly to CSOs—including NGOs, community and FBOs, and the private sector—or

by granting funds to an intermediary organization with the financial and technical capacity to provide sub-grants to smaller institutions
- A component to disburse funds to the public sector, including ministries of health and other ministries[1]
- A component to provide funds to National AIDS Commissions (NACs).

MAP Funding Flows

From fiscal 2001 to 2006, the Africa MAP lent almost US$1.3 billion in commitments, or 47 percent of the Bank's cumulative investment in HIV and AIDS since 1989 (Görgens-Albino *et al.* 2007). From fiscal 2006 to the end of fiscal 2009, additional lending brought the total to US$2.2 billion.

The channels through which funds reach communities vary across countries. A typical situation is shown in figure A.1. The National HIV/AIDS Council is the intended primary recipient of funds at the country level. Funds flow from there to community-level implementers through intermediaries, which can include district and local governments, NGOs, private-sector service providers, and line ministries. Most of the intermediary organizations also implement their own HIV and AIDS activities, which are supported by these funds. This system typically involves numerous small transactions that require carefully-designed accounting procedures.

Variations exist to take country-specific situations into account (figure A.2). For instance:

- In Mozambique, funds from the World Bank are transmitted to both the NAC and the Ministry of Health.
- In Uganda, the NAC does not manage funds, but it normally approves disbursements across sectors. Funds to civil society actors are released at the central project level and decentralized to administrative districts.
- In Zambia, a MAP project unit was established to process proposals and disburse funds received from the Ministry of Finance to the NAC and other ministries.

Funding to civil society and other sectors: Data on MAP's funding of civil society come principally from estimates included in a review of its first phase from 2001 to 2006. At that time, MAP estimated that 39 percent of MAP funds reached civil society (figure A.3). The disbursed funds intended for civil society implementers amounted to US$502 million across 31 countries, plus four multi-country projects in Sub-Saharan Africa.

The recipients included more than 66,000 CSOs and 234 line ministries. A significant variability is likely among recipients, but the report's figures indicate that the average annual allocation amounted to just over US$1 million for a line ministry and US$4,500 for a CSO. While the amounts provided to individual CSOs have been small, the number of CSO recipients has been relatively large. This approach distinguishes MAP's priorities from other more traditional projects.

Figure A.1 World Bank MAP's Typical Funding Flow

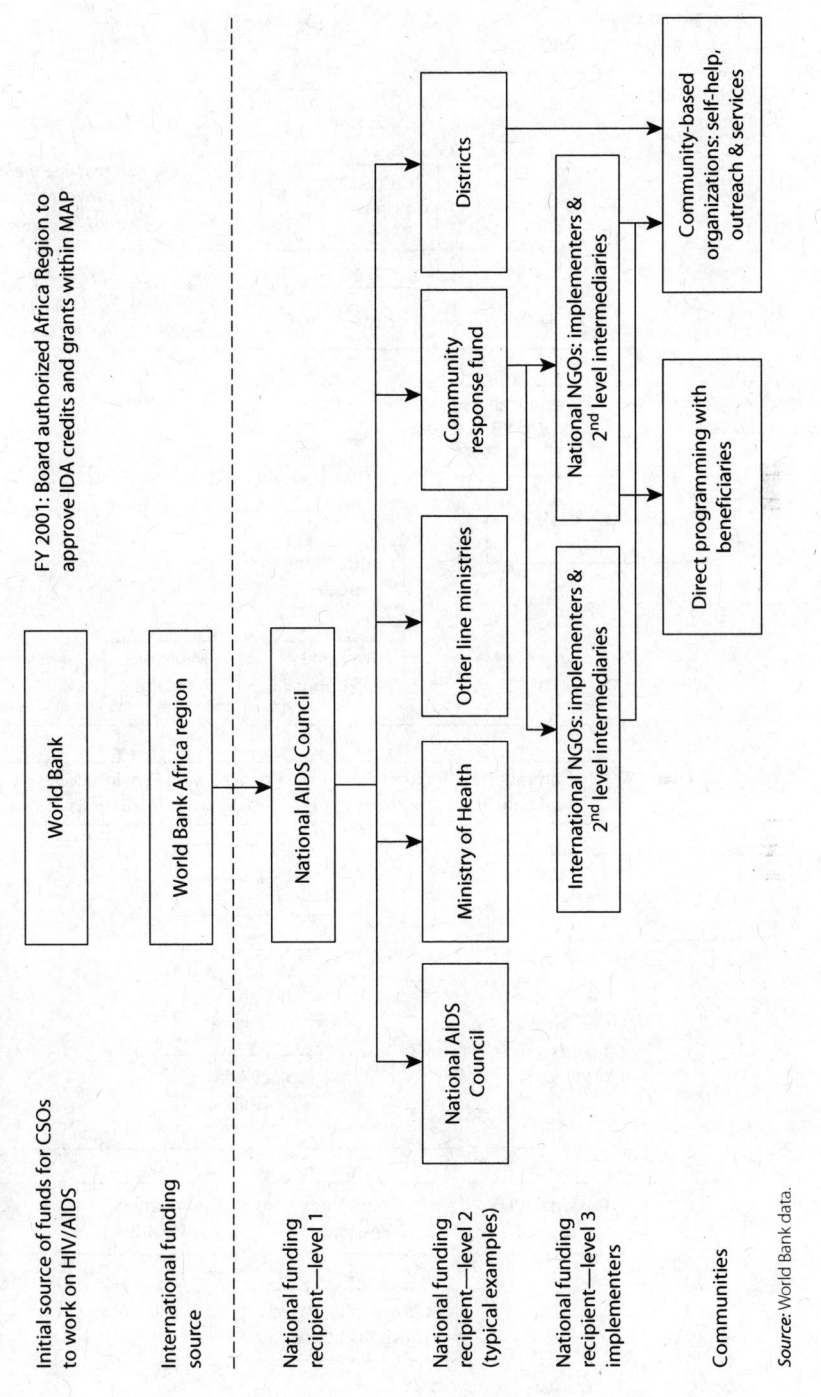

Initial source of funds for CSOs to work on HIV/AIDS	World Bank
International funding source	World Bank Africa region — FY 2001: Board authorized Africa Region to approve IDA credits and grants within MAP
National funding recipient—level 1	National AIDS Council
National funding recipient—level 2 (typical examples)	National AIDS Council; Ministry of Health; Other line ministries; Community response fund; Districts
National funding recipient—level 3 implementers	International NGOs: implementers & 2nd level intermediaries; National NGOs: implementers & 2nd level intermediaries
Communities	Direct programming with beneficiaries; Community-based organizations: self-help, outreach & services

Source: World Bank data.

33

Figure A.2 Variations on MAP Structures in Three Countries

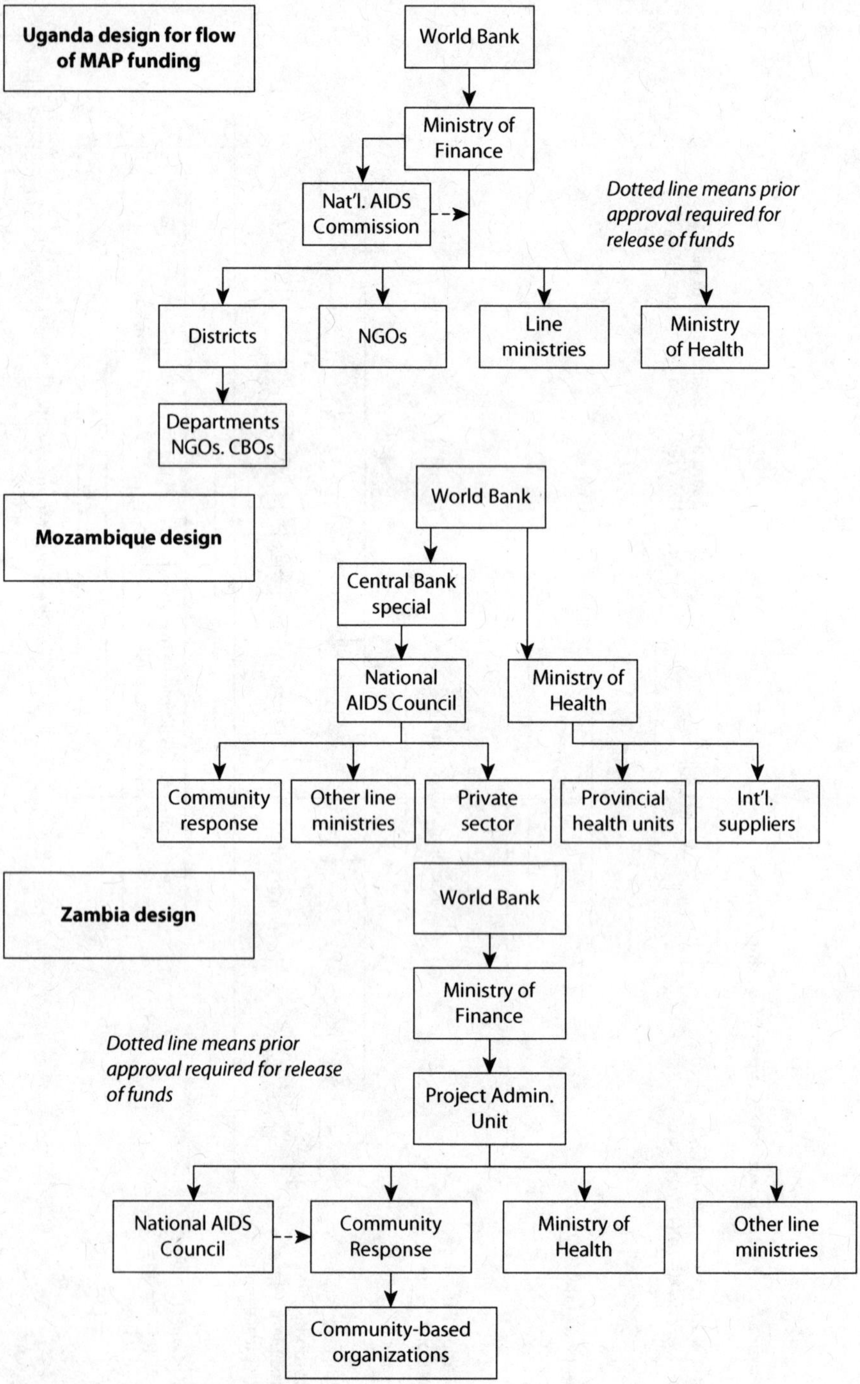

Uganda design for flow of MAP funding

World Bank → Ministry of Finance → Nat'l. AIDS Commission (dotted line)

Dotted line means prior approval required for release of funds

Ministry of Finance → Districts, NGOs, Line ministries, Ministry of Health

Districts → Departments NGOs. CBOs

Mozambique design

World Bank → Central Bank special → National AIDS Council
World Bank → Ministry of Health

National AIDS Council → Community response, Other line ministries, Private sector

Ministry of Health → Provincial health units, Int'l. suppliers

Zambia design

World Bank → Ministry of Finance → Project Admin. Unit

Dotted line means prior approval required for release of funds

Project Admin. Unit → National AIDS Council, Community Response, Ministry of Health, Other line ministries

National AIDS Council ⇢ Community Response

Community Response → Community-based organizations

Source: Oomman, Bernstein, and Rosenzweig 2007.

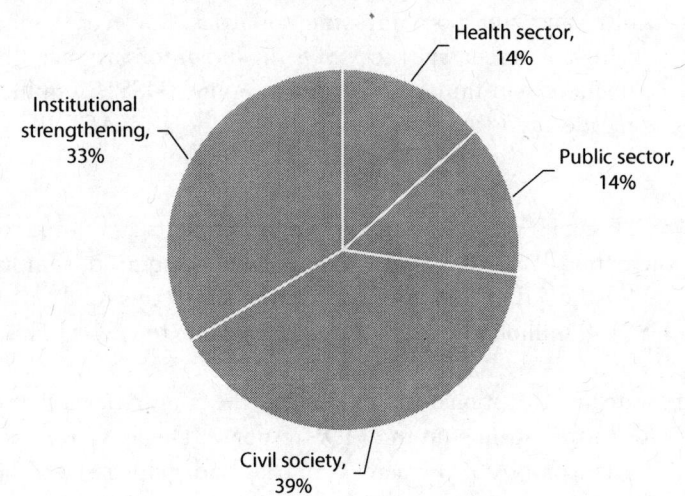

Figure A.3 World Bank MAP Estimated Disbursement (as of September 2006)

[Pie chart showing:
- Health sector, 14%
- Public sector, 14%
- Civil society, 39%
- Institutional strengthening, 33%]

Source: Görgens-Albino *et al.* 2007.

The MAP program was also innovative in that it included different types of organizations involved in community response and also funded institutional strengthening. Oomman, Bernstein, and Rosenzweig (2008a) concluded that the MAP's funding of different sectors of recipients, rather than funding of specific AIDS activities, resulted in increased capacity.

How sector recipients allocated funds: The Bank's report (Görgens-Albino *et al.* 2007) provides a breakdown of the MAP's disbursements by sector and activities for the period up to 2006, as follows:

- Health ministries allocated 62 percent of funds designated for their use toward HIV testing, management of sexually transmitted infections, and prevention of maternal-child transmission, and 19 percent was allocated for treatment.
- CSOs received most of the total prevention funding for activities such as peer education, promotion of condom use, and promotion of testing for HIV and other sexually transmitted infections. A quarter of all the disbursements to CSOs were for activities focused on care, treatment, and impact mitigation.
- Non-health ministries were given allocations mostly for prevention and for care activities, often aimed at government employees.
- National AIDS Councils used funding for institutional strengthening, coordination, research, monitoring and evaluation, capacity building, and operational costs.

The MAP design proved successful in scaling up the Bank's AIDS response across the Africa region. A similar approach was adopted in other geographic units of the Bank. HIV and AIDS financial assistance was provided either through stand-alone HIV and AIDS projects or as a component of projects in education, health, and transport. In some countries, however, Bank projects allocated even higher percentages to CSOs. In India, for instance, the World Bank project finances two-thirds of the total amount (US$150 million out of US$250million) allocated to prevention under the India's NACP III.

Key Findings

In total, World Bank HIV and AIDS project commitments amounted to US$3.4 billion for the period 1989–2010 with US$1.5 billion disbursed from June 2003 to June 2009 for the AIDS response worldwide. Out of this total, an estimated average of US$100 million per year was made available to CSOs.[2] This funding:

- Helped create an institutional environment at the country level that provided the basis for further scaling up the AIDS response: The MAP was responsible for the creation of NACs in many countries and helped strengthen those already in existence.
- Succeeded in promoting and facilitating a multi-sectoral response: It mobilized over 66,000 CSOs and 234 line ministries across Africa to become involved in the HIV response (Görgens-Albino *et al.* 2007).
- Helped build the community response to HIV and AIDS: World Bank funding for HIV and AIDS has also been the only substantial source of external support that local governments could access for strengthening their AIDS response.

The Global Fund to Fight Aids, Tuberculosis, and Malaria

International assistance for HIV and AIDS received a major boost when the Global Fund to Fight AIDS, Tuberculosis, and Malaria (Global Fund) was established in 2002. It was created in response to the nature of the HIV epidemic, which was viewed as an exceptional epidemic that deserved an exceptional response. The Global Fund was meant to address the following three key objectives:

- **Improving access to HIV and AIDS services:** When the Global Fund was founded, there was increasing global awareness of the AIDS burden in developing countries. Few countries, however, were in a position to scale up their response in order to provide a comprehensive program of HIV and AIDS services. At that time, UN agencies estimated that almost 30 million people were living with HIV, mostly in Sub-Saharan Africa, with almost 2 million people a year dying of AIDS (Oomman *et al.* (2008b)). Scaling up the global response was projected to require between US$7 billion and US$10 billion by 2005, an amount that far exceeded the resources that had been mobilized (UNGASS 2001).
- **Mobilizing adequate financing:** There was a widespread expectation that the creation of a new institution dedicated to attracting funding from a variety of

sources would be an effective mechanism for providing the financial resources needed for scaling up national responses to HIV and AIDS.
- **Applying a new development model**: The Global Fund was designed to represent a new development model in which, on the one hand, all stakeholders would be involved in developing a national response to HIV and AIDS and, on the other hand, disbursements would be based on the results that were achieved.

Funding Design and Funding Flows

The Global Fund's financial support for the AIDS response is spread across 144 countries, different HIV and AIDS activities, and different sectors of funding recipients and implementing agencies. In its 2010 report, the Global Fund stated that it provided US$7.3 billion in disbursements for HIV and AIDS from 2002 to end-2010. This amount represents 21 percent of international funding for HIV (Global Fund 2011).

From a recipient's perspective, the funding flow reflects four notable characteristics:

- **Provision of grant funding is based on the principle of country ownership**. Each country is responsible for creating a CCM. CCMs are country-level partnerships that include representatives from both the public and private sectors, such as governments, multilateral and/or bilateral agencies, and people living with HIV. Funding proposals are developed and transmitted by the CCMs for approval to an independent review committee—the Technical Review Panel (TRP). The TRP consists of 35 members, including disease and development experts.
- **Country proposals can include more than one top-level principal recipient (PR)**. For each grant, the CCM nominates one or more public or private organizations to serve as a PR. The PR is responsible for implementing the grant agreement and overseeing grant sub-recipients. The PR also has the task of developing a two-year agreement, including the results to be achieved.
- **The Global Fund is a financial rather than implementing agency**. Unlike traditional aid donors, the Global Fund was designed as a financing institution rather than an implementing entity. This principle influenced its initial design. For example, the Global Fund is active in 146 countries but does not have country offices in the countries that receive its grants. Instead, the Global Fund relies on the selected grant recipients for implementing the chosen interventions and mobilizing technical assistance, if needed. In addition, it relies on advice from local auditors referred to as Local Fund Agents (LFA). In the initial phase of the grant, the LFA's role is to assess the capacity of a nominated PR to administer grant funds and be responsible for implementation. Once the grant implementation starts, the LFA's task includes verifying the PR's disbursements and progress updates. The overall disbursement mechanism is illustrated in figure A.4.

Figure A.4 Global Fund Grant Process

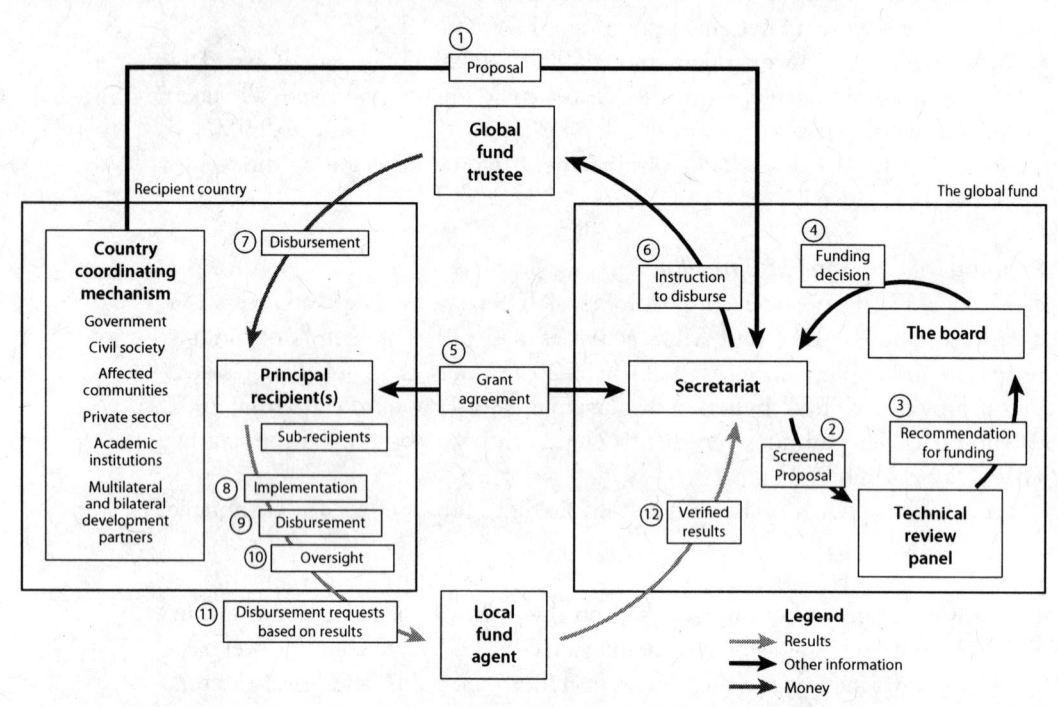

Source: Debrework Zewdie, Global Fund. Powerpoint presentation, at a seminar organized by the UK Consortium on AIDS and international Develpoment 2010.

- **Program plans are managed by many recipients.** Programming plans are often developed by different actors, then tied together into a single proposal that is accepted in its entirety, provisionally approved pending changes, or rejected. However, once funding agreements are signed, each recipient is responsible for its own program's performance. Each signs a grant agreement directly with the Global Fund and submits further disbursement requests directly to the fund's secretariat. Many recipients manage both program implementation and the disbursal of grants to other organizations.
- **The funding is performance based.** Initial funding is awarded solely on the basis of the technical quality of applications, but continued and renewed funding is dependent upon proven results and targets achieved. The first phase of funding lasts two years, and the second phase normally runs another three years. Approval for the latter, and any subsequent funding, is directly dependent on phase one performance, including outputs, numbers of beneficiaries, and the rate of spending against the original budget.

Funding through, and to Civil Society

The Global Fund's reporting systems provide information by type of implementing agency. One-third of reported expenditures for HIV and AIDS, tuberculosis, and malaria was spent by CSOs (Global Fund 2011). Applying

Table A.1 Funding Flows through Civil Society as Principal Recipients of the Global Fund's HIV and AIDS Grants (February 2003–June 2010)

	Number of civil society PRs	Number of grants	Total approved grants (US$)	Disbursements (US$)
Active grants	50	53	$947 million	$601 million
Closed grants	26	34	$541 million	$474 million
Lifetime grants	69	87	$1,488 million	$1,075 million

Source: Global Fund grants—progress details. Report generated for this report June 2010.

this percentage to the amount disbursed for HIV and AIDS (US$7.3 billion from 2002 to 2010) suggests that CSOs received US$300 million on average per year. This estimate includes the funds directly received by CSOs as Principal Recipients as well as the funds transmitted to CSOs through other channels such as government ministries.

Another source of information is provided by the analysis of the funding reaching CSOs as first-line recipients. Global Fund data indicate that 69 CSOs acted as PRs for the national AIDS response from February 2003 to June 2010. With some further research into the identity of organizations named in the data, it is possible to classify these PRs either as international NGOs or as nationally or regionally based organizations. This data indicates that US$1.1 billion was disbursed to civil society PRs, representing 18 percent of all disbursements for HIV and AIDS by the Global Fund.[3] Some 57 percent of disbursements to civil society PRs have been to national organizations, while international NGOs have received 43 percent of these transferred funds.

It should be noted that the funding reaching CSOs as PRs underestimates the funding received by civil society. To the extent that government PRs transmit some of the funding they receive to CSOs as sub-recipients, the total funding available to civil society would exceed the amounts shown in table A.1. For this reason, the alternative method of using CSOs expenditures to estimate the funding available for funding community responses is a more accurate method.

Regional Allocations

The regional distribution of HIV and AIDS funds from the Global Fund during the period of February 2003 to June 2010 is shown in figure A.5. The regional disbursements that have gone through CSOs as first-level PRs are shown in figure A.6. While 55 percent of all Global Fund disbursements are to programs in Sub-Saharan Africa, only 37 percent of these funds go through civil society PRs. By contrast, Eastern Europe and Central Asia have received 11 percent of the Global Fund's disbursements, but 39 percent of the these funds go through civil society PRs.

In West and Central Africa, the proportion of disbursements through civil society PRs is 19 percent, and in East Africa CSO PRs have received 13 percent of the regional funding. In southern Africa, a small number of CSO first-line recipients have received 8 percent of the total funding disbursed.

Figure A.5 Disbursements by Region
percent of lifetime disbursements February 2003–June 2010

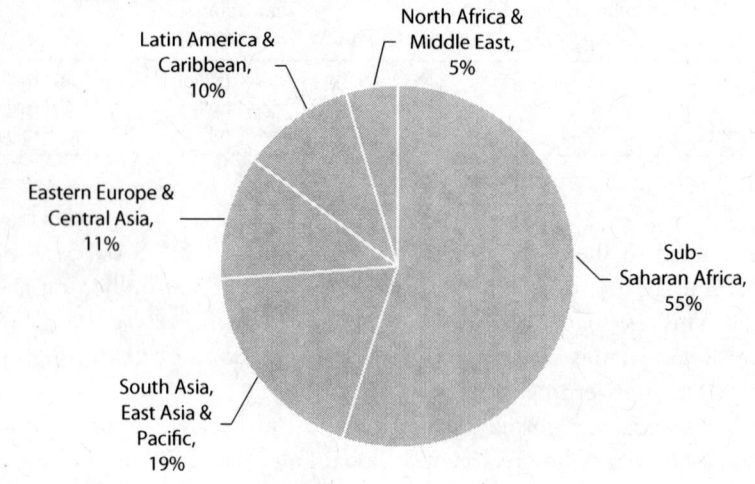

- North Africa & Middle East, 5%
- Latin America & Caribbean, 10%
- Eastern Europe & Central Asia, 11%
- South Asia, East Asia & Pacific, 19%
- Sub-Saharan Africa, 55%

Source: Global Fund 2011.

Figure A.6 Disbursements to CSO PRs
percent of life time disbursements; February 2003–June 2010

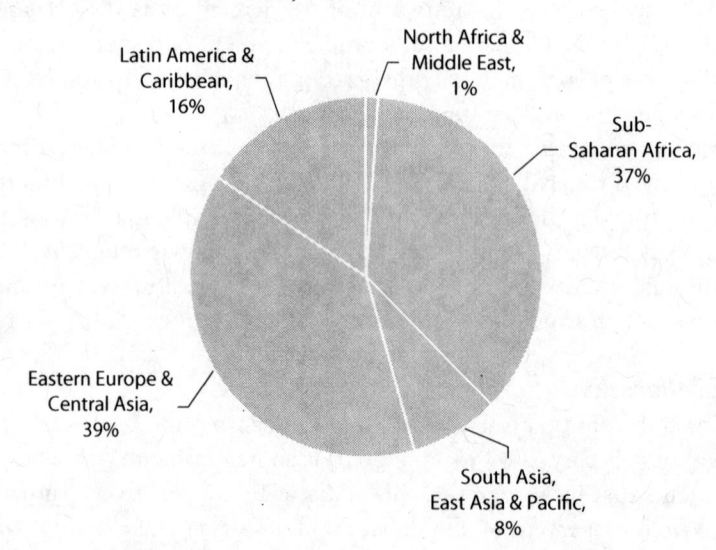

- North Africa & Middle East, 1%
- Latin America & Caribbean, 16%
- Sub-Saharan Africa, 37%
- Eastern Europe & Central Asia, 39%
- South Asia, East Asia & Pacific, 8%

Source: International HIV/AIDS Alliance.

Emerging Issues and Developments

Dual-track Financing

The relatively small role played by CSOs as PRs is an emerging issue. Obstacles have included government reluctance in many countries to work with civil society, which has obstructed both effective proposal design before funding and the management of grants once they are awarded (International HIV/AIDS Alliance and Global Fund 2008). Equally, there are barriers among CSOs, particularly local ones, in that they may not understand what they can propose to the Global Fund. In addition, members of the CCMs do not always understand the Global Fund's rules and procedures. For instance, they may believe that funding ceilings prevent the submission of more ambitious proposals that might include broader participation from civil society service providers and people in need.

In response, starting in 2008, the Global Fund did not require, but recommended, that all country proposals routinely include both governmental and nongovernmental PRs (Global Fund 2008a).[4] The first grants under this dual-track financing were signed starting in 2009. As a result, around 40 percent of PRs have been CSOs in rounds 8 percent and 9 percent compared to 23 percent during the seven previous rounds.

Capacity and Institutional Strengthening
The lack of capacity of CSOs has been a second emerging issue. Implementers at community levels are frequently challenged by a lack of resources for implementing community support activities, for human resources, and for monitoring and evaluation. In response, and parallel to the Global Fund's dual-track financing at the PR level, the Global Fund started to accept funding proposals for strengthening civil society systems in 2008 (Global Fund 2008a).

The Global Fund felt that the subsequent response in country proposals demonstrated a commitment to strengthening community systems. In total, between 50 percent and 80 percent of all the funding requests submitted in 2009 proposed reinforcing capacity in the following five areas: (1) scaling up or strengthening programming, (2) monitoring and evaluation, (3) partnership building, (4) strategic planning and management, and (5) financial management and reporting.

Single Stream of Funding
Important, from the point of view of recipients, the Global Fund has continued to review and modify its funding process. As the demand for financing increased rapidly, it reached a point where simplifying grant approval processes became essential to ensure that both approvals and the management of the grant portfolio remain efficient. Under the current Global Fund system, each approved proposal results in a separate grant agreement. And, under the new grant architecture approved by the Global Fund's board in November 2009, there is a single stream of funding for each recipient per disease. Grants are, thus, consolidated, which allows grant recipients to move away from a fragmented, project-type approach toward a program-based approach.

Implementation of this new architecture started in 2010. As part of the transition, countries are able to consolidate grants for round 10 on an optional basis. In 2011, single-stream applications will be rolled out for round 11.

National Strategy Applications

The creation of national strategy applications (NSAs) is another important change. While the Global Fund plans to retain specific funding rounds, NSAs are intended to provide an alternative to grant-by-grant funding. This approach makes it possible for countries to apply for financing on the basis of their national disease strategy (for example, National AIDS Strategy). A first wave of five NSAs was launched in 2009. It was followed by a second wave of NSAs in 2011. Expected benefits from NSAs include (1) improved alignment of Global Fund financing with countries' priorities, program cycles, and budgetary calendars; (2) improved harmonization with donors that use similar criteria for providing funding; and (3) national strategies that focus on managing for results.

Key Findings

- The Global Fund's institutional design has made it possible for national CSOs to access funding. While money has usually been disbursed to national governments, selected PRs have also come from the civil society sector. In total, civil society has received one-third of Global Fund disbursements during the 2002–10 period, which amounts to about US$300 million in disbursements per year.
- National CSOs have managed 57 percent of the funding disbursed to all CSO PRs, and international CSOs have managed the remaining 43 percent. This design reflects a trade-off between selecting recipients that can implement programs quickly (which are often international organizations) and selecting national organizations that may have lower capacity but offer a more sustained engagement over the long term.
- The Global Fund has reached a crucial turning point. Its philosophy of country ownership is evident in its recent decisions, especially the introduction of a dual-track funding mechanism and the National Strategy Application (NSA). CSOs, however, have not played the same role in all regions, which reflects different methods of choosing PRs within the country proposal mechanism and the different capacities of CSOs to prepare and implement proposals. With the introduction of dual track financing, the number of civil society PRs is increasing. This may result in increased access by a greater number of CSOs, but may also put an additional burden on the Global Fund to build the capacity of these recipients to manage funds efficiently. Similarly, the introduction of the NSA funding mechanism will allow the Global Fund to provide funding on the basis of a national AIDS strategy, but it is also likely to require strengthening governance and fiduciary systems.

US President's Emergency Plan for AIDS Relief (PEPFAR)

PEPFAR represents the first systematic attempt by a donor country to reverse the course of the HIV epidemic in low-income countries. The United States launched the first phase of the program in January 2003, with an initial funding authorization of US$15 billion for a five-year period. On June 2008, the PEPFAR program got a substantial boost as President George W. Bush approved a funding authorization amounting to US$48 billion to combat the global HIV epidemic, tuberculosis, and malaria; US$37 billion of this amount was directed to AIDS programs. Spending more than doubled between the end of fiscal 2005 and 2007 and more than doubled again by the end of fiscal 2009 (US PEPFAR 2006, 2008, 2010). This development has resulted in significant funding flows, with almost US$25 billion made available through various congressional appropriations and US$17 billion spent in the six years to the end of September 2009. The United States is the world's largest donor, accounting for more than half (58 percent) of disbursements by governments in 2009.

PEPFAR Design and Results

PEPFAR was initially designed as an emergency response focused on achieving quantified targets within a relatively short period of five years. This meant that the resources would be substantial, concentrated in the 15 most affected countries (12 of which are in Africa) and that implementation would have to proceed quickly.

In creating PEPFAR, Congress identified specific targets to be reached at the end of the five-year period. Since progress against these targets was the principal way that PEPFAR's performance would be assessed, a major focus was initially put on selecting implementers that had the capacity to deliver results quickly. Given the lack of implementation capacity in the low-income and heavily affected countries that were PEPFAR's focus, most of the implementation was carried out by international NGOs (mainly U.S.) with proven track records. Although some funds were transferred to a few recipient governments, most of the management was carried out by U.S. Government personnel. This approach ensured that funds would flow quickly and be disbursed in a manner that satisfied the accounting requirements of the U.S. Government.

PEPFAR achieved substantial results and met its objectives. Box A.1 contains a summary of results, which provide a good sense of PEPFAR's focus on outputs and the number of people reached.

PEPFAR's design reflected an explicit trade-off. A much greater weight was attached to the objective of achieving results quickly and in a manner consistent with the U.S. fiduciary requirements compared to the objective of building up a national AIDS response by strengthening the capacity of national governments and systems. The first objective was the most important, but it certainly carried the risk that the AIDS response might not be sustainable over the long term. This consideration influenced PEPFAR's new orientations in 2008.

> **Box A.1**
>
> **PEPFAR Results**
>
> Antiretroviral treatment was provided to more than 3.9 million men, women, and children as of September 2011
>
> PEPFAR supported nearly 13 million people affected by HIV and AIDS with care and support, including 4.1 million orphans and vulnerable children
>
> In FY2011, PEPFAR supported programs for prevention of mother-to-child transmission for more than 660,000 women, which allowed nearly 200,000 babies to be born HIV-free
>
> In FY2011, PEPFAR supported HIV counseling and testing for more than 40 million people as a critical entry point to prevention, treatment, and care
>
> *Source:* US PEPFAR 2011a.

New Orientation

In creating PEPFAR, Congress specified how it would allocate its funding. For instance, Congress specified that PEPFAR should use 55 percent of its funds for treatment, 20 percent for prevention, 15 percent for care, and 10 percent for OVC. PEPFAR also imposed other restrictions on the type of interventions that could be funded.

These restrictions were modified in PEPFAR's renewal with the objective of increasing flexibility. The 2008 reauthorization act did not specify in detail how the money should be spent, but it mentioned a few guidelines:

- Over half of the funds are to be spent on treatment programs, including antiretroviral treatment, care for associated opportunistic infections, and nutritional support for PLWHA.
- In countries with generalized HIV epidemics, at least half of all money directed toward preventing sexual HIV transmission should be for activities promoting abstinence, delay of sexual debut, monogamy, fidelity, and partner reduction.
- 10 percent for helping OVC.

In addition, some of the rules that had proven controversial were relaxed, especially related to abortions, condom use, and needle and syringe exchange.[5] These and other interventions became eligible for funding. The effect of these changes can be seen in the fiscal 2010 budget (figure A.7). Treatment comprised 36 percent of planned expenditures, including purchases of antiretroviral drugs, laboratory infrastructure, and adult and pediatric treatment delivery. About 27 percent of funds were planned to be spent on care and 36 percent on prevention.

The most important changes concerned PEPFAR's design. In the initial authorization Act, PEPFAR was designed as an emergency program with a focus on reversing the course of the HIV epidemic and scaling up treatment. Overtime, however, it became clear that the HIV epidemic had become a

Donor Funding Flows

Figure A.7 PEPFAR Fiscal 2010 Planned Funding for Prevention, Treatment and Care

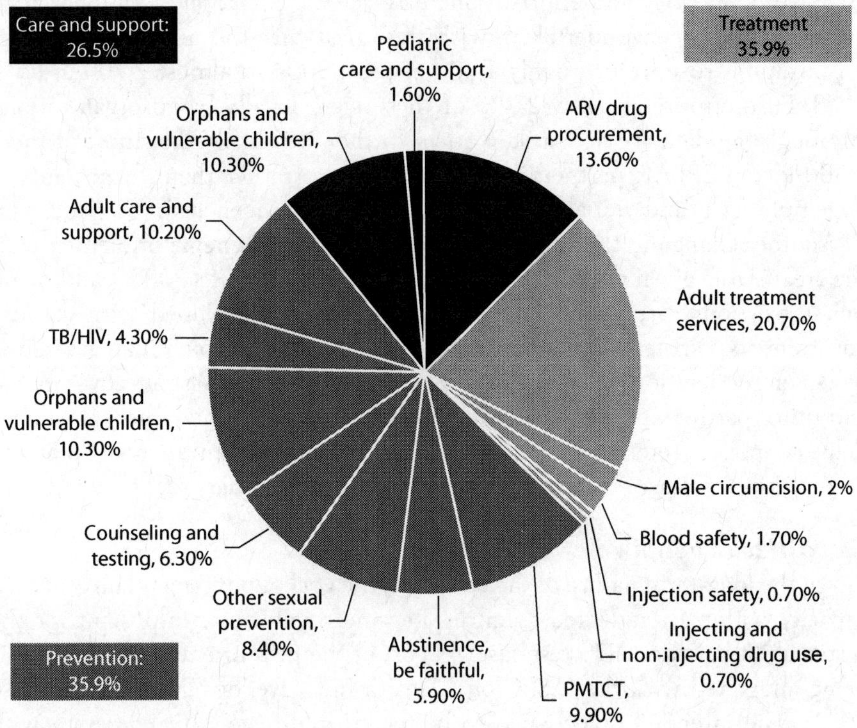

- Care and support: 26.5%
- Treatment: 35.9%
- Pediatric care and support, 1.60%
- Orphans and vulnerable children, 10.30%
- ARV drug procurement, 13.60%
- Adult care and support, 10.20%
- Adult treatment services, 20.70%
- TB/HIV, 4.30%
- Orphans and vulnerable children, 10.30%
- Male circumcision, 2%
- Counseling and testing, 6.30%
- Blood safety, 1.70%
- Other sexual prevention, 8.40%
- Injection safety, 0.70%
- Abstinence, be faithful, 5.90%
- Injecting and non-injecting drug use, 0.70%
- Prevention: 35.9%
- PMTCT, 9.90%

Source: PEPFAR 2011b.

chronic disease that would not be cured in the short term. This consideration motivated a reassessment of PEPFAR's goals and instruments.

In PEPFAR's second phase, a new program strategy is underway that supports an overall emphasis on improving country ownership, increasing program sustainability and integration, and strengthening health systems. Key new directions include the following.[6]

- Ensuring that PEPFAR programs are aligned with national AIDS strategies and integrated with existing health-care delivery systems
- Strengthening dialogue concerning the AIDS epidemic and its linkages with broader health and development issues
- Expanding technical assistance and capacity building to strengthen health systems
- Implementing expanded partnerships with governments, NGOs, and other stakeholders at country level.

Country Ownership

Since 2003, there have been attempts to adjust the overall program's partnerships. Notable among these changes are the following ones: First, single organizations can receive a maximum of 8 percent of a given country program's funding.[7] Second, efforts to increase the participation of national organizations have been undertaken, with the result that the number of partner organizations rose from roughly 1,600 in fiscal 2004 to almost 2,700 in fiscal 2008. Furthermore, roughly 2,300 of these were locally based organizations. Although the data are not broken down further, it is likely that most of these 2,300 local PEPFAR partners are national CSOs (rather than, for instance, a large number of individual government ministries or agencies).

Another change to the funding architecture currently being implemented is the greater role given to countries. As mandated in PEPFAR's 2008 reauthorization legislation, Partnership Frameworks have been developed with country governments. Partnership Frameworks provide a five-year joint strategic framework for cooperation between the U.S. Government, the partner government, and other partners to combat HIV/AIDS in the host country through service delivery, policy reform, and coordinated financial commitments. Some 21 Partnership Frameworks have been developed as of February 2011.[8]

Global Health Initiative

Given the long-term nature of the epidemic, the goal of building up institutional capacity within the affected countries became much more important for the sustainability of the AIDS response. As part of the new orientation, PEPFAR is being integrated with the U.S. Global Health Initiative, or GHI (White House 2009). The intended objective is to better integrate the AIDS program with support for the global health sector more broadly. As announced in May 2009, the administration's intention is for PEPFAR financing for HIV and AIDS and tuberculosis to constitute more than 70 percent of the GHI funds during a six-year period. The White House announcement also included specific projected funding figures through September 2014, as shown in table A.3.

While funding for PEPFAR more than doubled every two years since its inception, it is now slowing down. Congressionally approved AIDS funding was essentially flat-lined for fiscal 2010 from the previous year, within an overall annual increase of about 5 percent for the various components now making up the GHI[9] (Kaiser 2010a). Specific projected funding figures through September 2014 are shown in table A.2.

Table A.2 Projected US Global Health Funding (2009–14, US$ billions)

	FY2009 enacted	FY2010 budget	Six-year total (FY09–FY14)
PEPFAR (Global HIV/AIDS & TB)	$6.490	$6.655	n.a.
Malaria	$0.561	$0.762	n.a.
PEPFAR & Malaria subtotal	**$7.051**	**$7.417**	**$51**
Global health priorities subtotal	$1.135	$1.228	$12
Global Health Initiative total	**$8.186**	**$8.645**	**$63 billion**

Source: White House 2009.
Note: n.a. = Not applicable.

Funding Flows by Sources and Recipients

PEPFAR is managed by a number of implementing agencies and departments, but the vast majority of the funds go through the U.S. Agency for International Development (USAID) and the Centers for Disease Control and Prevention (CDC). As illustrated by figure A.8, the flow of funds is complex. Most recipients at country level receive their funding directly from the in-country field offices of U.S. agencies ("country-managed" funding), but another source of funding comes directly from U.S. agencies (such as, for example, CDC). Some of these country-level recipients may implement programs themselves, while others my transfer part of the funding to other sub-recipients.

Funds managed by U.S. Government agencies are generally not used by those agencies to implement AIDS activities directly. Rather, these agencies make awards to external entities, especially NGOs, universities, and private contractors. Funds to first-level recipients are awarded, for the most part, to U.S.-based organizations that implement HIV and AIDS activities directly (for example, through field offices), or are subcontracted to others. Sub-awards can go to a variety of organizations for activities in the field, including international NGOs or private contractors, as well as national CSOs in developing countries.

Across all sectors, international organizations appeared to meet the requirements to quickly handle large sums of funding. National organizations are perceived to suffer from insufficient capacity in financial management (specifically accounting, managerial and administrative skills, and auditing practices).

Funding to Civil Society Organizations

PEPFAR does not usually provide disaggregated information on the use of funds at country level. Some information was, however, gathered from the data obtained by the AIDS Monitor for fiscal years 2004–06. This data was analyzed by Oomman, Bernstein, and Rosenzweig (2008a) for the 15 focus countries.[10] Some of the key findings included the following:

- 71 percent of funding was intended for international NGOs.
- Only 19 percent of funds awarded to first-line recipients were subsequently sub-awarded to second-line recipients. On average, in these 15 countries, slightly more than half of these second-line recipient funds were granted to domestic organizations across all sectors. However, given the small total amount of sub-awards, second-line recipients received only 11 percent of the total funds that were received by the first line recipients.
- On average, 30 percent of funds were obligated to locally based recipients across the PEPFAR focus countries (again, across all sectors and not just civil society). The proportion of funding allocated to domestic agencies also varied considerably across countries. In four countries—Botswana, South Africa, Namibia, and Uganda—PEPFAR's obligations to domestic institutions ranged from 45 percent to 55 percent of the total.

Figure A.8 PEPFAR Funding Flow, October 2003 through September 2009

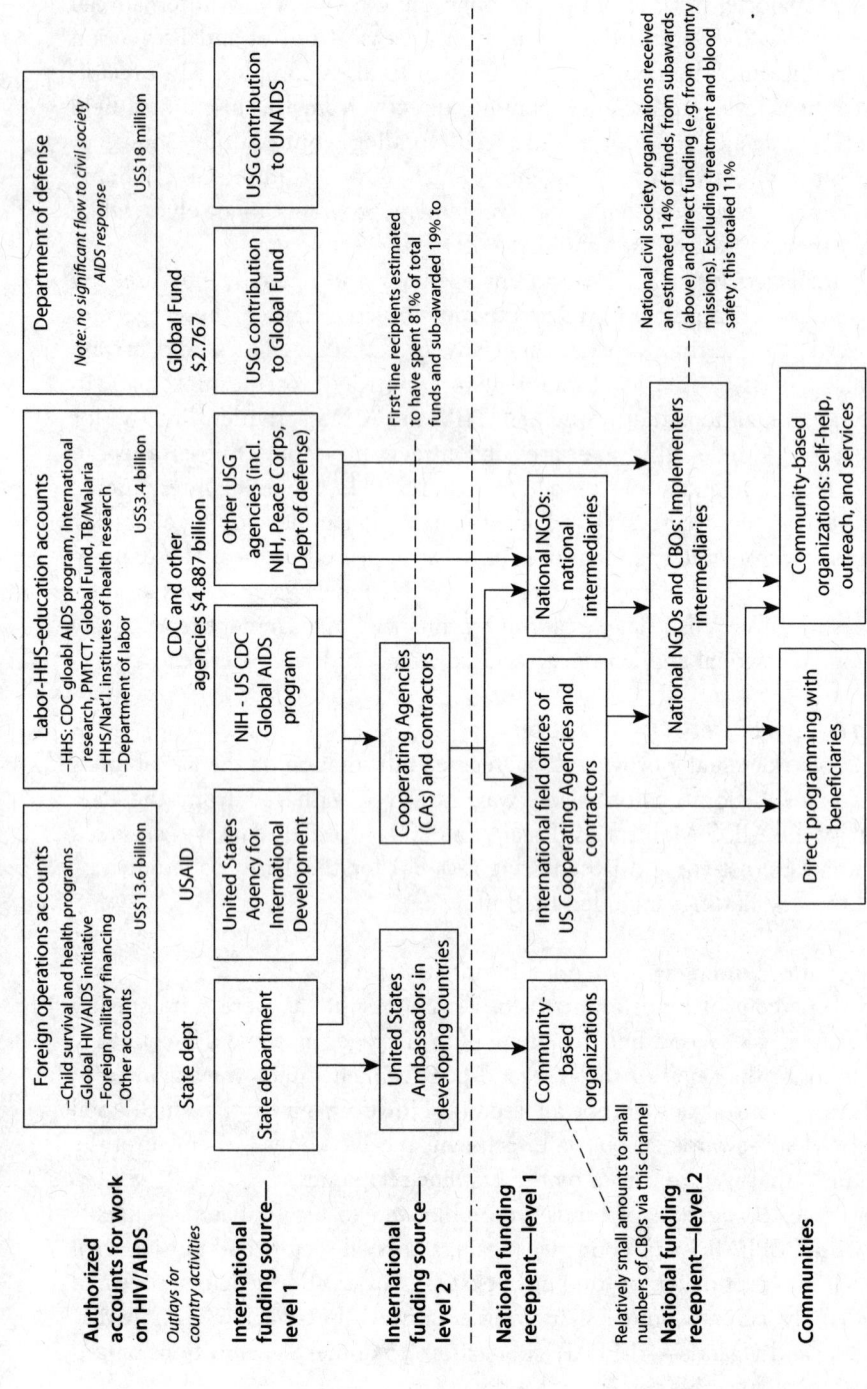

Authorized accounts for work on HIV/AIDS
Outlays for country activities

- **Foreign operations accounts**
  - Child survival and health programs
  - Global HIV/AIDS initiative
  - Foreign military financing
  - Other accounts
  US$13.6 billion

- **Labor-HHS-education accounts**
  - HHS: CDC global AIDS program, International research, PMTCT, Global Fund, TB/Malaria
  - HHS/Nat'l. institutes of health research
  - Department of labor
  US$3.4 billion

- **Department of defense**
  Note: no significant flow to civil society AIDS response
  US$18 million

International funding source—level 1

- State dept
- USAID
- CDC and other agencies $4.887 billion
- Global Fund $2.767
- USG contribution to UNAIDS

- State department
- United States Agency for International Development
- NIH – US CDC Global AIDS program
- Other USG agencies (incl. NIH, Peace Corps, Dept of defense)
- USG contribution to Global Fund

International funding source—level 2

- United States Ambassadors in developing countries
- Cooperating Agencies (CAs) and contractors

First-line recipients estimated to have spent 81% of total funds and sub-awarded 19% to

National funding recipient—level 1

- Community-based organizations
- International field offices of US Cooperating Agencies and contractors
- National NGOs: national intermediaries

Relatively small amounts to small numbers of CBOs via this channel

National funding recipient—level 2

- National NGOs and CBOs: Implementers intermediaries

National civil society organizations received an estimated 14% of funds, from subawards (above) and direct funding (e.g. from country missions). Excluding treatment and blood safety, this totaled 11%

Communities

- Direct programming with beneficiaries
- Community-based organizations: self-help, outreach, and services

Source: International HIV/AIDS Alliance analysis of funding flows.

- International and domestic FBOs received a small proportion of PEPFAR funds, with only 12 percent of funding obligated during 2005. About half of these funds were for treatment. Overall, more than 70 percent of funds obligated to faith-based CSOs went to three organizations: the U.S.-based NGO Catholic Relief Services, the Mission for Essential Drugs and Supplies in Kenya, and the international NGO World Vision.

Funding to National CSOs

Further analysis of the AIDS Monitor dataset was carried out to obtain estimates of PEPFAR funding flows to all CSOs, as well as to national CSOs at country level. There are various ways of analyzing the existing data, such as how amounts are allocated to international and indigenous CSOs.

Overall, our analysis indicated that spending plans for fiscal 2004–06 included obligations of 68 percent to be allocated to CSOs. If this percentage is applied to the actual outlays for PEPFAR country activities from October 2003 through September 2009 (US$12.4 billion), it results in an estimate of US$8.4 billion allocated to international and national CSOs. This figure includes clinical services run by nonprofit organizations or their implementing partners. When these are excluded, the total funding handled by CSOs can be estimated at US$7.4 billion during the fiscal 2004–09 period.

Analysis of the AIDS Monitor dataset further indicated that 14 percent of PEPFAR obligations were intended for national CSOs during fiscal 2004–06. Excluding clinical activities of treatment and blood safety, the flow to national CSOs can be estimated at 11 percent of spending plans. Applying this percentage to the period fiscal 2004–09 suggests that the funding of national CSOs for nonclinical activities amounted to US$230 million a year on average during the period fiscal 2004–09 (table A.3).

Expenses on HIV and AIDS activity areas by different CSOs: To get a sense of funding flows for types of HIV and AIDS activities implemented by CSOs, the data were further sorted to show only known net funding obligations for treatment, prevention, and care activities carried out by international and domestic nonprofit organizations.[11] For a general picture, the activity areas are

Table A.3 Estimated PEPFAR Funding for National CSOs

Funding flow and subsets: FY04–FY09	Total six-year outlay	Average per year
Total to country HIV/AIDS activities	$12.4 billion	$2.07 billion
Total for all types of CSOs: NGOs, universities, and faith-based organizations (68% of country programming)	$8.42 billion	$1.4 billion
Total for all CSOs net of treatment and blood safety (60% of country programming)	$7.43 billion	$1.23 billion
Total for national civil society organizations (11% of country programming)	$1.36 billion	$230 million

Source: International HIV/AIDS Alliance; PEPFAR data.

Table A.4 Distribution of CSO Funding by Activity Type (FY2004–06)

AIDS activity type	International CSOs (%)	Domestic CSOs (%)	All CSOs (%)
Treatment	48	42	47
Prevention	27	26	27
Care	25	32	26
Total obligations to types of CSOs	100	100	100

Sources: PEPFAR obligations, from AIDS Monitor project, Center for Global Development.

consistent with overall PEPFAR funding allocation: treatment was the most important, representing almost half of the funds, followed by prevention and care (table A.4). Compared to international organizations, national CSOs were allocated a higher proportion of their funding for care activities and a lower proportion for treatment.

Key Findings

PEPFAR was designed with a strong emphasis on meeting legislatively mandated, program-wide targets on prevention, treatment, care, and support. The emphasis on targets led PEPFAR to prioritize speed and the achievement of targets over other objectives, such as the sustainability of the AIDS response. As a result, most of the funds have been managed by large U.S.-based international CSOs with proven implementation records. This design has allowed PEPFAR to scale up the HIV and AIDS response rapidly and achieve substantial results.

As few national organizations in the low income countries that PEPFAR focused on were in a position to implement PEPFAR programs, little money has reached national CSOs. In total, they have received about US$230 million per year on average, amounting to 11 percent of PEPFAR country program funding.

After seven years of implementation, PEPFAR has now reached a turning point. It is undergoing a substantial transformation aimed at integrating the AIDS response within health sectors and strengthening national systems. This new orientation focuses on ensuring that the AIDS response remains sustainable over the long term.

DFID, United Kingdom

In recent years, the United Kingdom has become the second largest bilateral donor for HIV and AIDS, after the United States, and DFID primarily carries out these funding activities. DFID's first AIDS strategy, Taking Action, was launched in 2004 and committed the UK to spending at least US$2.5 billion in three years.[12] By 2008, DFID was spending close to US$1 billion annually on HIV in developing countries (Kaiser 2010b).[13]

As it launched its first strategy, DFID became a significant donor to the Global Fund, UNAIDS, and the United Nations Population Fund (UNFPA). It also engaged in efforts to leverage other sources of funding, and it successfully helped prod the G8 and the European Union to increase financial commitments in 2005. Some of these commitments went to new funding mechanisms such as UNITAID, whose mission is to achieve price reductions for diagnostics and medicines in developing countries.

The UK has increased its Official Development Assistance (ODA) in the past five fiscal years, including DFID's budget, which rose 66 percent from US$7 billion in 2004/05 to US$10 billion in 2008/09 (DFID 2009b). DFID's total spending on bilateral assistance consistently represented 40 percent of this total and, from 2004/05 through 2008/09, this assistance averaged US$5 billion per year. Apart from its bilateral aid, DFID has consistently spent US$3.5 billion on average per year (40 percent of its annual program funds) through its multilateral program. Some of these resources have funded HIV programs undertaken by CSOs. Additionally, in the above-noted period, $120 million per year went to the Global Fund and $20 million per year went to UNAIDS (DFID 2009a).

Funding Channels

DFID has a history of funding CSOs as partners in development. In recent years, DFID's annual direct funding of CSOs averaged US$610 million (12 percent of the total bilateral program expenditure[14]), with US$160 million granted to 30 organizations with Partnership Programme Agreements. An additional US$450 million was channeled through a number of central and country-based funding mechanisms that reach civil society partners. While this strategy was designed by the previous government, the new UK coalition government has kept the instruments/funding channels in place to support civil society. These include the following:

Partnership Programme Arrangements (PPAs): these are the most significant single channel of direct DFID funding to civil society. They provide flexible strategic support to CSOs from around the globe which share a common ethos and vision with DFID and which are able to show value for money and an ability to deliver against outcomes. In the latest round of PPAs, DFID agreed to fund 39 organizations, many of which work on HIV and TB.

Support to networks: these include those working on HIV prevention for most-at-risk populations, such as the Global Forum of MSM and Harm Reduction International.

The Governance and Transparency Fund (GTF): DFID created the £130 million GTF fund for helping citizens hold their governments accountable by strengthening the wide range of groups that can empower and support them. Currently, however, there are no plans to replenish this fund.

Civil Society Challenge Fund (CSCF): The CSCF for UK-based organizations supports activities that

- Improve the capacity of CSOs in the Global South to engage in national decision-making processes
- Improve national linkages through global advocacy

- Provide innovative service delivery, and
- Provide service delivery in difficult environments.

The CSCF can provide up to £500,000 for a maximum of five years. Projects for which UK organizations have secured a degree of funding from other sources, or are making a contribution of their own, are welcomed. However, up to 100 percent will be considered where no other funding is available.

The Global Poverty Action Fund (GPAF) was launched on October 27, 2010, with an expected start date in April 2011. The GPAF will be a demand-led fund that supports projects focused on service delivery to reduce poverty. It will also focus on poor countries that are the most off-track of the Millennium Development Goals. Projects will be selected on the basis of a demonstrable impact on poverty, clarity of outputs and outcomes, and value for money.

DFID, both in the UK and through country offices, uses these various channels to provide funding to civil society. From its UK office, DFID channels centrally managed funds through approximately 330 CSOs, but country offices can also provide support to CSOs. For instance, they have created their own Civil Society Challenge Funds and can channel funds through civil society via supply contracts that are tendered for specified services or deliverables. Country offices have also supported basket fund programs, which are country-based financing mechanisms intended to increase development assistance that is harmonized with the Paris Declaration on Aid Effectiveness.[15] The visual map of DFID's funding flow is summarized in figure A.9.

Civil Society Spending on HIV and AIDS

As yet, there is no available data set that provides information specifically on AIDS spending by civil society recipients. However, DFID recently released a database of projects (amounting to US$38 billion) that were active in August 2009, or have started since then. This database was used to estimate the funding received by civil society.

To provide a reasonable estimate, only CSO projects that include "HIV" in their title or description were taken into account. A first category of projects includes those in which HIV is a principal focus. These account for 6.8 percent of the funding for CSOs. In addition, there is another set of CSO projects for which HIV was coded as a "significant" part of their efforts (rather than either "principal" or "not targeted"). These represent another 2.4 percent of the CSO funding. Applying these percentages to the overall expenditure through CSOs in past years indicates that spending on HIV projects amounted to an annual average of about US$56 million for the years 2004/05 through 2008/09 (table A.5). During the same period, DFID disbursements for HIV and AIDS amounted to about US$3.3 billion (US$587 million per year on average), based on the annual estimates provided by Henry J. Kaiser Family Foundation (Kaiser 2010b). This suggests that CSO funding amounted to about 10 percent of total HIV and AIDS funding.

Figure A.9 DFID Funding Flow

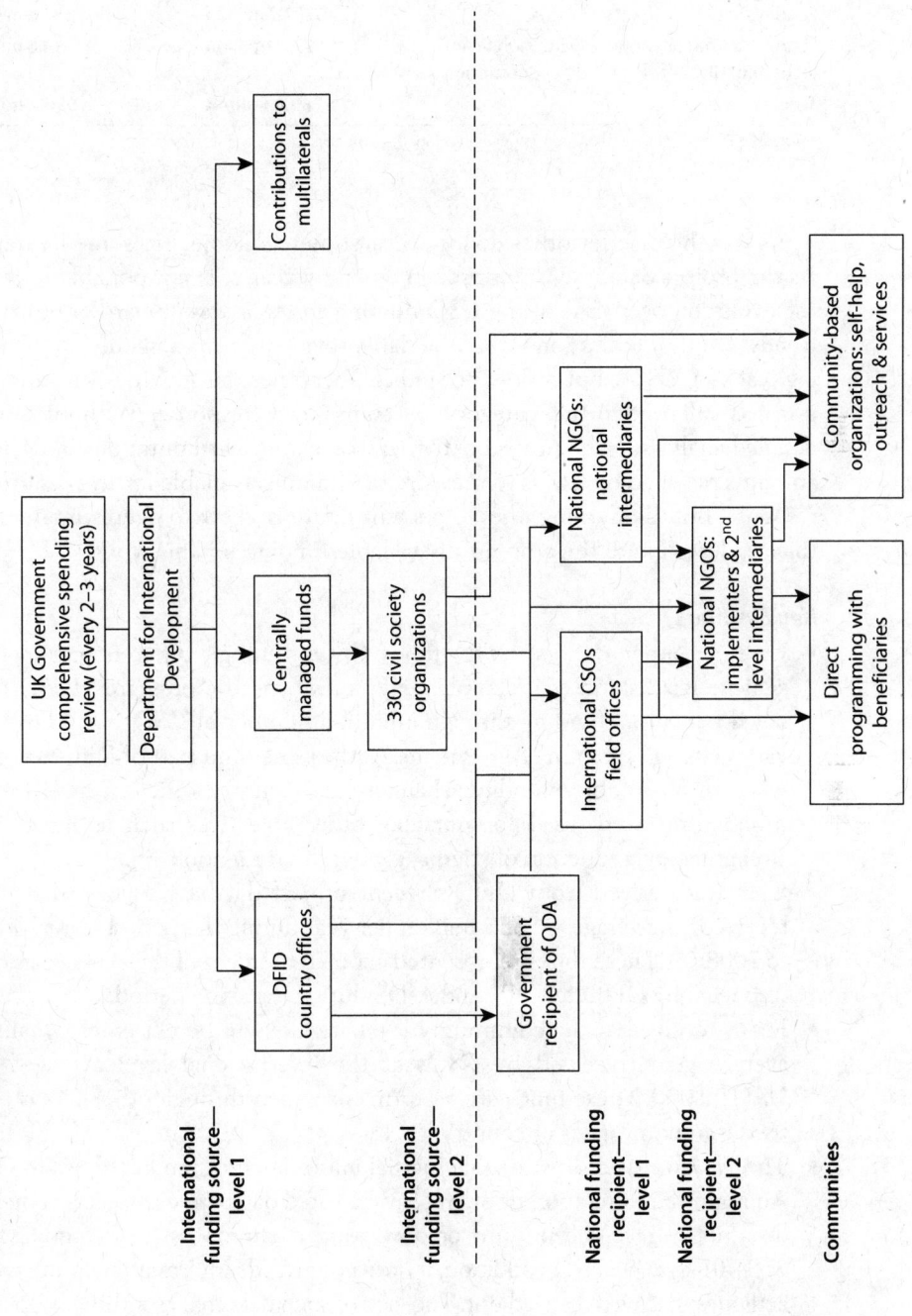

International funding source—level 1
- UK Government comprehensive spending review (every 2–3 years)
- Department for International Development
- DFID country offices
- Centrally managed funds
- Contributions to multilaterals
- 330 civil society organizations

International funding source—level 2
- Government recipient of ODA
- International CSOs field offices
- National NGOs: national intermediaries

National funding recipient—level 1
- National NGOs: implementers & 2nd level intermediaries

National funding recipient—level 2
- Direct programming with beneficiaries
- Community-based organizations: self-help, outreach & services

Communities

Source: International HIV/AIDS Alliance.

53

Table A.5 Estimated CSO Budgets with Principal or Significant HIV Focus

	Estimated CSO funding in FY2004/05 to FY2008/09	Average per year
Funding with "principal" HIV focus	$207.9 million	$41.6 million
Funding for mixed projects: with "significant" focus and "HIV" in title or project description	$72.9 million	$14.6 million
Total	**$280.8 million**	**$56.2 million**

Sources: DFID "Project Information" (report generated June 7, 2010); DFID 2009a.

As was the case for other donors, this estimate is subject to some limitations. As the project database is not broken down by year, it is not possible to retrace the evolution over time of the CSO funding and to assess upward or downward trends. Another limitation is that the data provide information only on the funding reaching CSOs, but it does not indicate whether the activities that are being pursued fall under the category of community response. Without a more detailed analysis of the project activities, there are clear limitations in using the amounts received by CSOs to measure the funding available for the community response. But, if anything, the 10 percent figure is likely to overestimate rather than underestimate the amount of available funding for this work.

Key Findings

- Case for other donors, DFID funds CSOs through different channels. To achieve results and quick implementation of specific programs, DFID channeled part of its funding through a limited number of CSOs, i.e., those with Partnership Programme Agreements. At the same time, part of DFID's funding went through other funding channels like country offices. These funding mechanisms were used for pursuing other objectives such as institutional strengthening, reduction of stigma, gender discrimination, etc.
- Estimates derived from DFID's recent project database suggest that CSOs received, on average, US$56 million per year during the period from 2004/05 to 2008/09. These funds represented about 10 percent of the average amounts disbursed by DFID for HIV and AIDS during the same period.
- Funds received at the community level are likely to be extremely small. The average grant received by CSOs at the international level averaged only US$170,000. These funds are, in turn, channeled through other CSOs or are used to fund projects at country level.
- The available data provides only partial information of funding flows to CSOs. An important limitation of the recently created database of projects is that it is does not retrace the upward or downward evolution of CSO funding from 2004/05 to 2008/09. In addition, it does not provide information on the type of activities that were carried out. The lack of such data makes it difficult to assess the extent to which this funding supports community response activities and/or benefits people living with HIV.

Notes

1. Some MAPs (Burundi, Ethiopia, and Ghana) did not have such a component because they received parallel financing provided through a World Bank health project.
2. This assumes that 39 percent of the total AIDS funding went to CSOs, as was the case for the MAP projects.
3. For this study we considered "active grants" to be those signed with PRs and scheduled to last beyond March 2010; these data do not include grants awarded in 2009, since the PRs had not been confirmed and were awaiting grants signature in mid-2010.
4. It was a recommendation rather than a requirement, but the Global Fund further stipulated that applications without a CSO proposed as a PR should provide reasons and discuss alternatives for ensuring both governmental and nongovernmental implementation.
5. In the case of needle and syringes, new guidance was issued in July 2010.
6. These changes are described in PEPFAR's five-year strategy, available at www.pepfar.gov/strategy.
7. Three exceptions to this rule are: funding to the government, to an organization procuring commodities related to treatment, and to organizations managing umbrella funds to smaller organizations.
8. See www.pepfar.gov/frameworks.
9. As well as HIV and AIDS, this now includes: tuberculosis, malaria, the Global Fund, child survival and maternal health, vulnerable children, family planning and reproductive health, avian flu, and neglected tropical diseases.
10. These include 13 countries in Africa—Botswana, Côte d'Ivoire, Ethiopia, Guyana, Kenya, Mozambique, Namibia, Nigeria, Rwanda, South Africa, Tanzania, Uganda, and Zambia—as well as Haiti and Vietnam.
11. Net obligations are allocations received by an agency and not onward granted. The distribution of AIDS activity budgets by type of CSO is based on net obligations to known recipient types. These were coded both by geographic origin of the recipient and by activity area and total $1.29 billion. Although a subset of the total data, it was the portion that was most clear in its allocation by both geography and activity areas.
12. The actual commitment was £1.5 billion. Unless otherwise noted, this figure and other DFID funding figures are converted for this report at US$1.85 per British pound. This was the average interbank rate for fiscal 2004/05 to 2008/09, rounded.
13. This excludes its contribution to the Global Fund and UNITAID (US$78 million).
14. This was alongside 20 percent of bilateral spending through budgetary support to developing country governments, 20 percent through multilateral agencies (as managers or channels of specified bilateral aid), and the balance through other channels, including humanitarian assistance, technical cooperation (specialists, training, research), and other financial and bilateral aid.
15. From the point of view of civil society funding recipients, these mechanisms are defined by the fact that several donors contribute to pooled funds to which CSOs can apply from within the country, rather than directly through individual bilateral donor headquarters or country offices.

References

DFID (UK Department for International Development). 2009a. "DFID and Gross Public Expenditure on Multilateral Contributions 2004/05–2008/09." http://www.dfid.gov.uk/About-DFID/Finance-and-performance/Aid-Statistics/Statistics-on-International-Development-2009/Tables-index/. Accessed May 28, 2010.

———. 2009b. "DFID Expenditure on Development 2004/05–2008/09." http://www.dfid.gov.uk/About-DFID/Finance-and-performance/Aid-Statistics/Statistics-on-International-Development-2009/Tables-index/. Accessed May 28, 2010.

Global Fund (Global Fund to Fight AIDS, Tuberculosis and Malaria). 2008. "Fact Sheet: Dual-Track Financing." Global Fund Fact Sheet Series, 3 of 5, Global Fund, Geneva.

———. 2011. "Making a Difference: Global Fund Results Report 2011." The Global Fund to Fight AIDS, Tuberculosis and Malaria, Geneva.

Görgens-Albino, M., N. Mohammad, D. Blankhart, and O. Odutolu. 2007. *The Africa Multi-country AIDS Program 2000–2006: Results of the World Bank's Response to a Development Crisis.* Washington, DC: World Bank.

International HIV/AIDS Alliance and Global Fund. 2008. *Civil Society Success on the Ground: Community Systems Strengthening and Dual-Track Financing—Nine Illustrative Case Studies.* Hove, UK: International HIV/AIDS Alliance and Geneva: Global Fund.

Kaiser (Henry J. Kaiser Family Foundation). 2010a. *Budget Tracker: Status of U.S. FY10 Funding for Key Global Health Accounts.* Menlo Park, CA: Henry Kaiser Family Foundation.

———. 2010b. *Financing the Response to AIDS in Low-and Middle-income Countries: International Assistance from the G8, European Commission and Other Donor Governments in 2009.* Menlo Park, CA: Henry Kaiser Family Foundation.

Oomman, N., M. Bernstein, and S. Rosenzweig. 2007. *Following the Funding for HIV/AIDS: A Comparative Analysis of the Funding Practices of PEPFAR, the Global Fund and Work Bank MAP in Mozambique, Uganda and Zambia.* Washington, DC: HIV/AIDS Monitor, Center for Global Development.

———. 2008a. *The Numbers behind the Stories: PEPFAR Funding for Fiscal Years 2004 to 2006.* Washington, DC: Center for Global Development.

———. 2008b. "Report on the Global Epidemic 2008." Geneva: UNAIDS.

UNGASS (United Nations General Assembly Special Session). 2001. *Declaration of Commitment on HIV/AIDS.* New York: United Nations.

US PEPFAR (US President's Emergency Plan for AIDS Relief). 2006. "Summary Financial Status as of September 30, 2005, Year Two of Implementation—Data Represents All of FY 2004 & FY 2005 through Q4." US Department of State, Washington, DC.

———. 2008. "Summary Financial Status as of September 30, 2007 (4th Quarter—FY 2007)." US Department of State, Washington, DC.

———. 2010. "Summary Financial Status as of June 30, 2009 (3rd Quarter—FY 2009): Data for FY 2004— 2008 Appropriations." US Department of State, Washington, DC.

———. 2011a. "Using Science to Save Lives: Latest PEPFAR Results." www.pepfar.gov/documents/organization/187770.pdf.

———. 2011b. "Seventh Annual Report to Congress (2011)." US Department of State, Washington, DC.

White House. 2009. *Statement by the President on the Global Health Initiative.* Washington, DC: White House.

APPENDIX B

Country Funding Profiles

India

India is an unusual case characterized by a heterogeneous epidemic. It has a low national HIV prevalence rate (0.3 percent of the adult population) but concentrated epidemics among most-at-risk population groups (in some states HIV prevalence rates exceed 1 percent). And because of the size of its population, it is home to the largest number of people living with HIV in any country outside of Africa (2.3 million). The NACP III[1] recognizes that providing outreach services in a country the size of India, and where the most-at-risk groups are marginalized, is difficult. It has therefore focused its prevention interventions among these groups, engaging them in the implementation of the program and relying on a diversity of institutional mechanisms that include public institutions, NGOs, CBOs, civil society, and private health institutions to deliver prevention, treatment, care, and support.

Civil Society Activities

The Indian Government has a long history of supporting CSOs, and their evolution has continued in recent years with the expansion of the AIDS response. There are numerous CSOs working on HIV and AIDS at the local, state, and national levels—between 1 million and 2 million according to some estimates.[2] These organizations represent an immense potential for building a strong AIDS response, which is explicitly acknowledged by NACP III.CSOs are viewed as playing a key role, particularly in preventive or targeted interventions for high-risk groups and care and support of PLWHA, and in general awareness building campaigns.

Under NACP III, there is an effort to expand **Targeted Interventions** (TI) for high-risk groups. These interventions are delivered by CSOs in partnership with the National AIDS Control Organization (NACO) and provide comprehensive and integrated services for HIV prevention among marginalized and vulnerable populations, such as female sex workers (FSWs), IDUs, men having sex with men (MSM), and bridge populations such as migrant workers and truck drivers.[3]

Given the perceived efficacy of CSOs in reaching the targeted population groups, NACP III seeks to increase their role at district, state and national levels to provide home-based care, set up community care centers for people living with HIV, and address stigma and discrimination. In 2006, CSOs were involved in 1,080 targeted intervention projects. Currently, there are 1,609 targeted interventions covering 1.1 million high risk groups (FSW, MSM and IDU) that are implemented by 2,200 CSOs (mainly NGOs).

Grassroots organizations are numerous and widely spread across the Indian states, but there is also a relatively small group of larger Indian and international NGOs that is receiving direct funding from donor agencies. Several of these NGOs act as intermediaries and provide sub-grants to grassroots organizations that work with smaller constituencies in one district or a cluster of districts. Through these various channels, implementation on the ground is almost entirely carried out by local NGOs and CBOs.

Funding Sources for Civil Society Aids Activities

There are several funding streams in India that reach CSOs in important ways. Some date back only a few years but have evolved considerably, notably through NACP III's expansion of the AIDS response since 2007; Avahan's scale-up of focused prevention up to 2009; the expansion of Global Fund support of civil society PRs; and the creation of a pooled fund with World Bank and DFID. In addition, support from bilateral and multilateral sources has continued with some changes in emphasis, such as alignment with government funding schemes that reach CSOs.

NACP III

The Indian Government's total budget for the NACP is almost US$2.6 billion for five years (2007–12). The main expected sources of funds are the following:

- Direct budgetary support (US$1 billion) provided by non-pooled funding, resources for condom procurement, and other programs
- Direct budgetary support coming from the pooled fund (US$898 million, the World Bank, DFID, and the Government of India)
- Extra-budgetary resources (US$676 million) that include funds from various development partners, such as the U.S. Government, the Bill & Melinda Gates Foundation, the Clinton Foundation, and other foundations (These resources also include Global Fund grants to NGOs, such as the Population Foundation of India, the India AIDS Alliance, Tata Institute of Social Science, and the Indian Nursing Council).

Some donors such as USAID and the United Nations Development Programme (UNDP) divide their funds between government and extra-budgetary channels, while others such as the European Commission and the Gates Foundation's Avahan do not use the government channel and fund CSOs directly.

Table B.1 First- and Second-line CSO Recipients of Key AIDS Funding Flows

Donor	Organizations	No. of CSOs
National AIDS Control Organization (NACO) and State AIDS Control Organizations (SACS), including DFID and World Bank as pooling partners	Local NGOs and CBOs implementing targeted prevention interventions	1,300
	NGOs implementing Link Worker outreach scheme (15 at state level and 125 at district level)	140
Global Fund	Mostly Indian NGOs and CBOs, some international NGOs	430
Avahan/Gates Foundation	Larger Indian and international NGOs Academic institutions Local NGOs and CBOs implementing targeted prevention interventions	160
USAID	Larger Indian and international NGOs Local NGOs and CBOs	150
European Commission	Indian and International NGOs	45
Total		2,225

Source: International HIV/AIDS Alliance.

Despite a common perception that international donors are the lead funders for CSOs, the Government of India probably supports the largest number of organizations carrying out AIDS activities, especially smaller CSOs at the district and state level. An example of the importance of the government's role is shown by a sample of key donors that funded CSO activities (table B.1). Based on this sample, the government provided funding to over half the 2,200 CSOs that received funding.

Bill & Melinda Gates Foundation's Avahan: Started in 2003, Avahan is an HIV and AIDS initiative of the Bill & Melinda Gates Foundation. Although Indian CSOs were already involved in targeted prevention activities for key populations with major investment provided by development partners (USAID, CDC, DFID, and World Bank), Avahan was the first initiative to follow a business model for scaling up prevention. Avahan funded CSOs to implement interventions for high-risk groups such as sex workers, their clients and partners, MSM, hijra and transgender people, and IDUs. Activities are in six high-prevalence states and along major trucking routes.

Avahan's overall funding flows to civil society have been relatively large, with the program spending more than US$200 million from 2003 to 2009. However, the Gates Foundation is phasing out its direct support to AIDS prevention in India. Interventions will continue to be implemented by Indian CSOs, but the government will increasingly assume financial responsibility. In total, NAC III forecast funding of US$317 million for this initiative.

Global Fund: Financing from the Global Fund has expanded over several years to include more civil society involvement. While the government was the sole first-line recipient of the first two AIDS grants to India, CSOs have been included in subsequent rounds. The more recent rounds appear to continue a trend to spend funds more widely through different CSO channels. From 2005 to the beginning of 2010, different Global Fund grants have disbursed US$54 million through CSOs acting as first-line PRs.

Pooled funding: The main focus of pooled funding has been to fund NGO and CBO interventions. Funding is provided by the World Bank (US$250 million), DFID, and the Indian Government. In total, the available resources for the pooled fund currently amount to US$508 million, with a funding gap of US$390 million during NACP III. In this context, the World Bank currently finances 55 percent of 1,609 targeted interventions implemented by CSOs. These interventions cover an estimated 1.1 million high-risk groups, and DFID finances the remaining 45 percent. CSOs are funded against the implementation of standardized programs and an agreed-upon set of deliverables. Assuming that the percentage of pooled funds allocated to the implementation of NGOs/CBOs interventions is the same as the World Bank's (60 percent), the estimated funding reaching small CSOs would amount to US$60 million per year.[4]

Other bilateral and multilateral donors provide direct financial support to civil society.

- **USAID**'s funding increased significantly, from US$11 million to US$15 million annually under NACP-II, to US$22 million annually under NACP III. Approximately two-thirds of this funding flows to CSOs, although a significant portion is now routed through the NACO programs.
- **DFID** resources for NACP-III have increased, but are now part of the pooled funds, apart from a small portion for a capacity-building project. Under NACP-II, DFID made 58 grants to CSOs under its Civil Society Challenge Fund, which provided about US$7 million from 2005 to 2007, but has now ended.
- **UNDP**'s annual commitments rose from roughly US$15 million under NACP-II to US$20 million under NACP-III, but the funding patterns have become much more aligned to NACP priorities, which limits the flexibility of direct funding for CSOs.
- There are some other funds from **foundations, charities, and international NGOs** that finance civil society activities, but usually at levels that are felt to be significantly smaller than the donor flows cited above.

With the available information, it is difficult to provide an accurate estimate of the funding flows that actually reach civil society in India. However, it is possible to provide an estimate. Most of the funding for national CSOs comes from the pool of funds noted above and direct funding from donors, which is classified as extra-budgetary resources. Simply adding the average annual funding provided by Avahan (US$63 million), the pool of funds (US$100 million), and the Global Fund (US$11 million) would total 31 percent of the NACP III funding that has been identified as being available.[5] Adding the funding provided by government and other bilaterals and foundations would further raise this share.

CSOs' expenditures on AIDS activities: It is not possible to obtain data that disaggregate expenditures by both activity areas and CSOs. As an alternative, feedback was elicited from a sample of 10 of the more prominent and active Indian and international NGOs. Their responses indicate that at least half, and probably more, of civil society's AIDS funds are likely being spent on prevention. This is in line with the Government's overall budget for the National AIDS Control Plan, which devotes two-thirds of its funding to various types of prevention activity. Respondents also indicated that some of their activity focuses on care and support of those directly affected and some focuses on impact mitigation work. Civil society advocacy activities were also mentioned, but spending in these areas appears to be relatively small.

Results-based Financing

India provides an example of how results-based financing has been applied to CSOs. Three important characteristics include (1) provision of results-based financing, (2) availability of assistance for capacity building, and (3) evaluation of results.

- **Provision of results-based funding:** Funding is provided against the implementation of standardized programs and an agreed-upon set of deliverables.
- **Building up the capacity of CSOs:** Donors are encouraged to fund Technical Support Units (TSUs) at national and state levels, with the intention of increasing the management capacity of CSOs and relying less on international agencies for technical assistance. The pooled funding established by the World Bank and DFID is an example of this policy. To enhance the quality of targeted interventions, the pooled funding is used to finance some of the 17 state TSUs and some of the 18 State Technical Resource Centers (STRC). These institutions provide guidance and monitoring services to CSOs (TSU), as well as training for the CSO implementers (STRC). Simultaneously, the NACO has strengthened the capacity of the STRCs through specific training programs and the provision of training manuals for various cadres of CBOs and NGOs.
- **Evaluation of results:** CSO's performance is evaluated annually. Their organizational capacity, financial management, and delivery of services are reviewed and used to measure their performance, which in turn is used for terminating or renewing their contracts.[6]

Key Findings

Indian NGOs/CBOs play a large role in the implementation of the national AIDS response. They are viewed as essential partners by the NACP III and, as a result, they have obtained access to funding for implementing targeted interventions for high risk groups.

Donor funding is aligned to government channels. With increasing alignment of donor flows to government-managed AIDS programming, the National AIDS Plan could eventually be the dominant stream of funding for CSOs.

The government has recognized the critical role of capacity building, in particular for CBOs. Capacity building results, in part, from the NACO, which has encouraged donors to fund Technical Support Units at national and state levels. The intention is to shift away from the use of international technical agencies. By making technical assistance available, as well as funding for building up their management capacity, CBOs are gradually being empowered to access results-based funding.

There are indications that interventions by small NGOs and CBOs can be effective. Evidence from the evaluation of India National AIDS Program showed that targeted interventions for female sex workers were cost-effective, amounting to US$100 per infection averted and US$11 per disability-adjusted life-years (Daly) averted. The evaluation estimated that the HIV prevalence among the adult population would be 0.25 percent and 0.48 percent, with and without FSW interventions, respectively (Prinja, Bahuguna, and Rudra 2011). The effectiveness of CBOs was further confirmed by two studies focused on assessing the role of CBOs for communities-at-high risk of infections (Mohan et al. 2011; Saggurti et al. 2011) that were carried out as part of the World Bank evaluation of the community response to HIV and AIDS in partnership with the Bill & Melinda Gates Foundation.

Civil society has played a role in ensuring complementary programming. This role has included advocacy for child-focused care and support and securing external resources for providing services to marginalized and hard-to-reach groups, such as IDUs and MSM.

Kenya

Kenya is experiencing a mixed and geographically heterogeneous HIV epidemic with characteristics of both a generalized epidemic among the general population and a concentrated epidemic among specific and most-at-risk populations. The HIV epidemic peaked in the late 1990s with an overall prevalence of over 14 percent in adults. Since then, the HIV prevalence rate declined to 7.1 percent in 2007 among the 15–64 year olds (Kenya National AIDS Strategic Plan 2009/10–2012/13).[7] Large variations exist among provinces, with the highest rates in the Nyanza province (16 percent). High-risk groups such as commercial sex workers or IDUs have even higher HIV prevalence rates of up to 30 percent.

Faced with such an epidemic, the Government of Kenya declared HIV and AIDS a national disaster in 1999, and subsequently established the National AIDS Control Council (NACC) in 2000 to coordinate the national response. Following the first Kenya National AIDS Strategic Plan (KNASP I), KNASP II (2005/06–2009/10) focused on three priorities: preventing new infections, improving the quality of life of people infected and affected by the HIV epidemic, and mitigating the socio-economic impact of the epidemic.

In 2009/10, Kenya's Government prepared and launched a revised plan (Kenya National AIDS Strategy Plan 2009/10–2012/13, or KNASP III). KNASP III continues the epidemiological priorities of KNASP II, but it adds a new dimension by focusing on strengthening program implementation via integration with different delivery systems. Accordingly, KNASP III is organized along four priority areas or implementation pillars, namely, (1) health sector HIV service delivery, (2) mainstreaming HIV by sector, (3) community-based HIV programs, and (4) governance and strategic information.

Implementation of these pillars is interlinked. For instance, interventions under pillar 1 (health sector delivery) are linked to pillar 3, which is aimed at strengthening local referrals to government services, building capacity of communities, and establishing quality assurance mechanisms. Pillar 3 recognizes that knowledge, demand, and utilization of services in the formal health system are highly dependent on a strong community-based advocacy and referral system.

Funding Kenya's National Response

The national AIDS response in Kenya has received significant funding from PEPFAR, DFID, the World Bank, and several other donors. In total, the available funding rose from US$418 million in fiscal 2006/07 to US$660 million in fiscal 2007/08 and US$687 million in fiscal 2008/09 (Kenya National AIDS Control Council. UNGASS 2010) (figure B.1) (UNAIDS 2010). Bilateral funding is the overwhelming source of support (75 percent) followed by government expenditures (14 percent) and funding from other international and multilateral

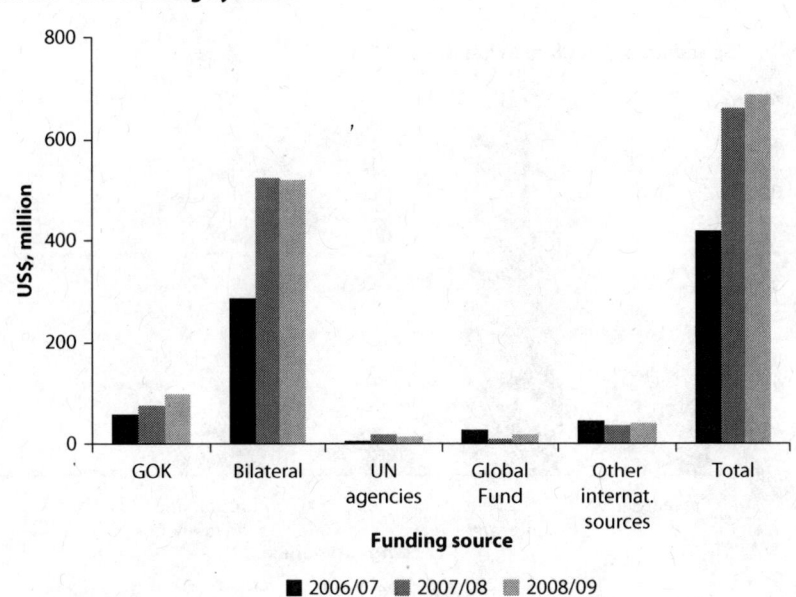

Figure B.1 AIDS Funding by Source

Sources: Kenya National AIDS Control Council, UNGASS country report 2010.

organizations (12 percent). Most of the increase in funding came from bilateral sources, especially PEPFAR.

The distribution of spending did not change much during the 2006–09 period. Treatment and care received the most funding (55 percent) followed by prevention (25 percent), program management (10 percent), and OVC (at 7 percent) (figure B.2).

Funds in Kenya were disbursed through two main funding mechanisms: the government budgetary system and off-budget channels. Funds disbursed through the government's funding channel included the government's own funds, funds provided by the World Bank TOWA project, and funds from the Global Fund's contribution to the Ministry of Health (as Principal Recipient). In total, public institutions managed about 45 percent of the available funding, NGOs 48 percent (mainly government and faith-based hospitals), and bilateral and multilateral institutions 7 percent (Kenya 2009).

Most of the external resources for HIV and AIDS are disbursed off-budget. Funding goes through donor-managed projects, or through NGOs without going through the government budget. Examples include funding provided by the Global Fund to Care International as the civil society PR, or funding provided by PEPFAR to large international CSOs. The reported data indicates that the bulk of funding received by CSOs came from the United States (through various channels), followed by funds from the United Kingdom.[8]

Donor funding for CSOs: Kenya has a relatively large number of CSOs, as well as Kenyan NGOs operating at provincial and national levels. There is also a fairly significant presence of international NGOs. Data from the 2009 KNASA indicates that out of 385 NGOs that formed the sampling

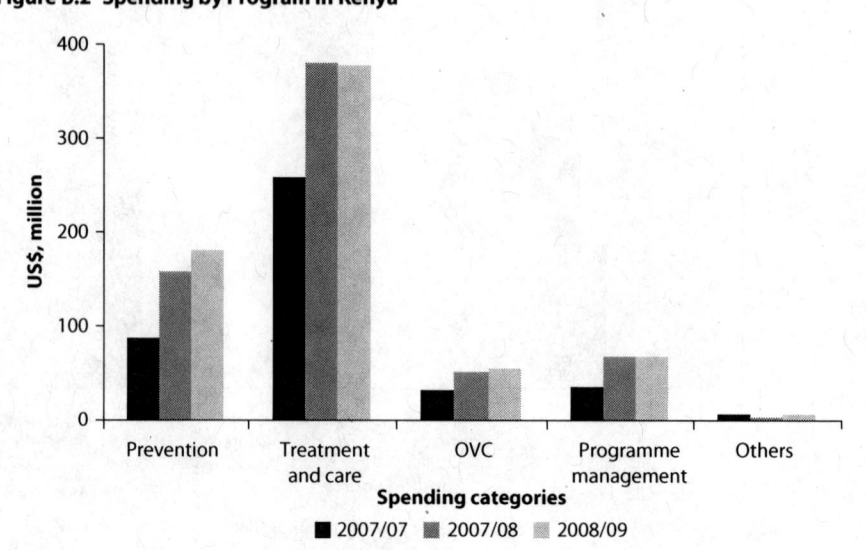

Figure B.2 Spending by Program in Kenya

Sources: Kenya National AIDS Control Council, UNGASS country report Kenya 2010.

frame of KNASA, 40 percent were international NGOs. Expenditures by CBOs were estimated to amount to only 2 percent of the 2007/08 national expenditures.

Recent Developments

Renewed importance of community response: A key orientation of KNASP III is the importance it attaches to community response. Policy and strategic reviews carried out during the preparation of KNSAP III showed that scaling up the national response requires increased provision of health services, but also better targeted CSO-implemented interventions.

The increased involvement of CSOs has been supported by donors. For instance, the follow-on to the Global Fund round 7 grant included the involvement of 34 CSOs alongside government implementers (Kenya CCM 2007). Access to the round 9 grant should further increase resources for CSOs.

The 2009 World Bank TOWA Project, which started disbursements in late 2008, also provides substantial HIV funding for CBOs. The Bank identified some 14 priority interventions, which provided the basis for issuing calls for proposals. So far, promising results have been achieved. As of August 2010, 2,225 project sub-implementers had been contracted and by August 2011, over 4,000 CBOs had received support. The funding amounts under the TOWA project are approximately US$3,500 for each grant award to the lowest level CBOs.[9]

This funding served to even an uneven playing field. As indicated by the 2009 KNASA, most of the donor funds for the community response at the national level were received by a few large CSOs and only a small fraction trickled down to lower level NGOs and CBOs. However, Kenyan's CBOs have been able to access national funds as well as donor aid. This conclusion comes from the 2011 evaluation of the community response in the Nyanza and Western Provinces of Kenya (World Bank 2011). Results from the 24 surveyed CBOs showed that national funding channels are providing their main source of funding. These included the Ministry of Health (23.7 percent), local government (19 percent), foundations and charities (8.7 percent), and funds generated by the CBOs themselves (2.6 percent) (figure B.3).

Perhaps surprisingly, external funding sources amounted to 46 percent of the total resources of the surveyed CBOs. This shows that contrary to a perception widespread in the literature on community organizations, Kenyans' CBOs are able to access international funding. By itself, this is good news. However, the large share of external funding suggests that CBOs may be vulnerable to its reduction. Mitigating this factor is the nature of the CBOs. The CBOs that were surveyed in Kenya's Nyanza and Western Provinces were found to employ on average 21 volunteers. The estimated value of unpaid volunteers' time represented over 40 percent of the resources of the CBOs.[10] This suggests that the vulnerability of CBOs to cuts in external funding is less than suggested by the

Figure B.3 Community-based Organizations in Western and Nyanza Provinces: Sources of Funding (2010)

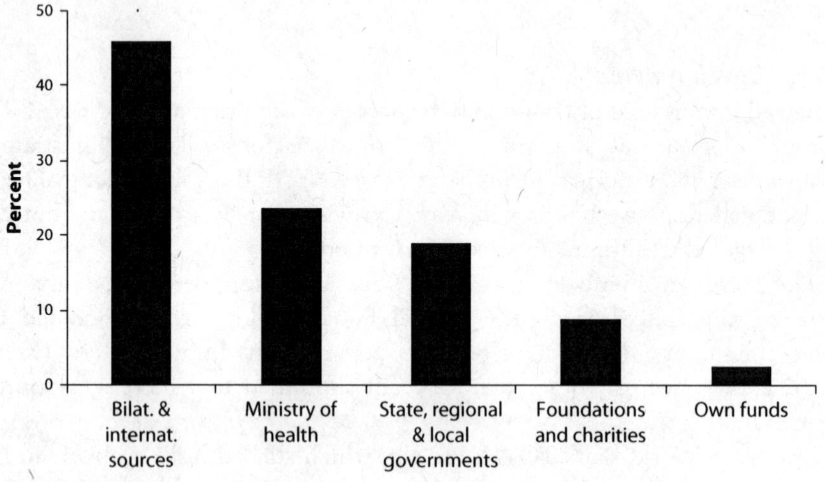

Source: World Bank 2011.

Table B.2 Spending of CBOs and National Program by Categories

	National AIDS Program (2007/08) (%)	Surveyed small CBOs (2010)2/ (%)
Prevention	26	28
Treatment and care	55	15
Impact mitigation	8	29
Program management & others	11	28

Sources: For column 1, Kenya National AIDS Control Council. UNGASS 2010; for column 2, World Bank 2011.

high percentage of external funding. Nevertheless, it seems unavoidable that CBOs are unlikely to maintain their HIV and AIDS activities without additional funding from the Government.

Activities of CBOs: The information provided by the surveyed CBOs showed the complementary role played by these organizations. Compared to the national response, proportionately more funds were spent on prevention efforts, impact mitigation, and program management and capacity building (table B.2).

Key Findings

Support for CBO activities is relatively small but growing. For 2008, the funding flow to civil society reported in the NASA amounted to 2 percent of the total HIV and AIDS funding. In later years, the financial resources available to CBOs have probably doubled due to funding provided by various institutions, including the World Bank TOWA project.

CSO activities complement or are substitutes for the national AIDS response. At the national level, international CSOs were able to access international funding due to their experience in implementing projects, disbursing funds quickly, and meeting reporting, monitoring and fiduciary standards. In these roles, these CSOs were substitutes for government. At the community level, small NGOs and CBOs tended to provide more a complementary role to the government, although there were also concerns that their role might extend to provide services that should be provided by government.

CBOs are able to access funding through various channels. But getting money to where it is needed is only part of the challenge. The value provided by CBOs is greatly dependent on two things: (1) the funds must flow where they would have the greatest impact on the HIV epidemic, and (2) if many of the small NGOs and CBOs are to become viable partners, they need stronger support directed at increasing their capacity to implement interventions that are effective by international standards. These objectives could be attained by selecting interventions for which CBOs have a clear implementation advantage compared to other institutions and then providing support through performance-based contracting.

As in other countries, it is difficult to monitor the funding received by CBOs in Kenya. The Kenyan Government has a long history of supporting CSOs, but capturing their activities, and documenting their role, would require significant additional effort. For instance, the 2009 KNASA sampled only 80 organizations, which appears low in view of the much larger number of NGOs that are listed in the database of Kenyan network of CSOs.

Peru

Peru's AIDS epidemic affects key populations. For instance, while pregnant women (a proxy of the general adult population of reproductive age) have an HIV prevalence rate of 0.2 percent, it is estimated that MSM have a national prevalence rate of 14 percent (Peru, Ministry of Health 2010). In total, 76,000 Peruvians are estimated to be living with HIV.

Donor Funding for Civil Society AIDS Activities

From 2006 to 2008, the total financing for AIDS in Peru across all sectors amounted to roughly US$112 million (Peru, Ministry of Health 2008, 2010).[11] During this period, 11 external donors provided US$30 million to CSO's for AIDS-related activities. Almost half of this funding was for health research projects carried out by NGOs. The Global Fund was the largest funding source for CSOs that were responding to the HIV epidemic, representing almost 35 percent of revenue for all of civil society's externally funded-projects (table B.3). Four health research centers were the next most important source of funds and accounted for 44 percent of funding. All of these centers are based in the United States and, presumably, were principally channeling centrally awarded U.S. Government research funding. Apart from the Global Fund, the European Union and USAID are the next most important official donors active in the country. According to USAID Peru, approximately US$1.5 million is granted

Table B.3 CSO AIDS Funding in Peru from External Sources (2006–08)

	All CSO funding (%)	Funding excluding health research projects (%)
Global Fund	35	62
Research institutes	44	0
European Union	7	12
International NGOs	9	16
USAID	5	10
Total	100	100

Source: Records of Peruvian Agency of International Cooperation (APCI) 2009.

annually, with resources channeled through U.S. organizations or contractors that have included Peruvian organizations as partners within their proposals. Some international NGOs also provide direct funding to Peruvian CSOs.

Funding for activities considered to be more typical of community AIDS responses are shown in the second column of table B.3, which excludes funding for health research. In total, US$17 million, or an annual average of US$5.7 million, was available for funding non-health-research activities of CSOs. This represents 15 percent of the national funding flow from 2006 to 2008 for HIV and AIDS.

Donor funding trends: International funding that reaches CSOs in Peru for all types of development work has increased slightly compared to funding of five to seven years ago, due, in part, to the creation of the Global Fund. Peru has received more Global Fund commitments than any other country in the region, or almost US$59 million in rounds 2, 5, and 6 for all sectors. The last two rounds have explicitly included CSOs, with significant funds to strengthen activities reaching vulnerable populations and for countrywide implementation.

Expenditures on Aids Activities

Most of the non-research activity carried out by 26 Peruvian CSOs from 2006 to 2008 was dedicated to prevention. The 26 organizations implemented 90 projects in this period, of which 60 were prevention projects and 14 were focused on health research. The main focus of prevention activities included decreasing sexually transmitted infections; providing comprehensive care for MSM and for sex workers; reducing social impact, stigma, and discrimination; and strengthening PLHIV organizations.

The CSOs' emphasis on prevention is in contrast with the allocation of expenditures for the national AIDS response. In 2006–08, 44 percent of national AIDS spending was for care and treatment and 29 percent for prevention.[12] While the epidemiological profile in Peru would indicate that focused prevention for key populations is a priority—notably for MSM, sex workers, and transgender people—the Peruvian Government does not intervene in these areas. Hence, CSOs are the main actors in the prevention field. At the same time, focused prevention activities are not found across all CSOs. Of the projects reviewed in this study, only 30 percent concern key populations.

In terms of treatment, the Ministry of Health has gradually taken over funding of antiretroviral therapy (ART) and, currently, almost all of these drug costs are provided free by the government (Visser-Valfrey, Cassagnol, and Espinel 2009). For prevention, the Government focuses on three activity areas: antiretrovirals for pregnant women living with HIV to prevent mother-to-child transmission, awareness for school groups (although not nationwide), and prevention campaigns oriented to the general public.

Civil society recipients of AIDS-related funding: Analysis of the 2006–08 data of the Peruvian Agency of International Cooperation (ACPI) shows that 26 CSOs received funding for AIDS activities, with about 70 percent of the funding concentrated in only five organizations. These CSOs were seen as having experience in project implementation and service provision. They received, on average, US$1.4 million per year with grants ranging from US$490,000 to US$3.8 million annually. The higher amounts were allocated to CSOs that concentrated on health research activities. The other 21 organizations, many of them relatively new, received, on average, US$140,000 per year during the past three years

Implementation of CSO AIDS activities in 2006–08 was for the most part carried out by national CSOs. International CSOs have been involved mainly as funders of Peruvian CSOs. This approach is different from the profile in other development areas, in which about 140 international CSOs both directly implement their own activities and also work with Peruvian NGOs and grassroots CBOs.

There is not a long history of Peruvian CSOs acting as intermediary organizations for AIDS funding. National CSOs work with grassroots groups, but the responsibility for managing financial resources, logistics, and supplier contracts is kept with the larger CSOs while the smaller CBOs carry out only agreed-upon activities. Out of all the CSOs working on AIDS, only one provides small prevention grants to CBOs. Generally, CBOs are viewed as lacking the capacity to produce project proposals and to manage them, with a few exceptions.

Efforts to change this situation started in 2006. NGOs and CBOs in Peru were explicitly included in the Global Fund's plans. Following the Global Fund requirement that at least one CBO from each recipient consortium be included in the round request, more CBOs started to become Global Fund sub-recipients. Four CSO consortia were formed, involving 17 CSOs in total. Each consortium is focused on four specific objectives: reducing sexually transmitted infections (STI), providing comprehensive care for MSM, reducing social stigma and discrimination, and strengthening organizations of PLWHA.

Additional efforts to decentralize CSO funding started in late 2007. This included increasing the number of organizations acting as fund managers and implementers. The process started with CARE assessing institutional capacities in each region. Eventually, CSO consortia were formed for each of the programmatic objectives in the north, central-south, and east of the country. A total of nine consortia involving 24 CSOs have been formed.

Key Findings

Funding for CSO activities (excluding health research) amounted to US$6.7 million per year, which was 15 percent of the total AIDS flow to Peru in 2006–08. Over 60 percent of this amount was provided by the Global Fund. Key informants described several positive impacts of the funding mechanism set up by the Global Fund. Namely, it included a coordination mechanism allowing for stakeholder discussion and prioritization; it included populations directly affected by HIV (which allowed for better consideration of their needs and for strengthening their organizations as institutional stakeholders); and it opened the possibility of joint work with other CSOs (which helped expand coverage of activities). In addition, there has been a learning process that has resulted in strengthening project management capacities.

Shortcomings of the funding include the following: dedicated staff is needed to fulfill a large number of reporting requirements; technical support is not provided for donor compliance; and the focus on quantitative monitoring does not allow for qualitative assessments. CSO staff is mobilized exclusively to achieve project goals, and there is uncertainty about the future once Global Fund financing ends.

There is a **diverse profile** among a relatively small number of CSOs that are involved in AIDS work, with funding concentrated among a few organizations. Intermediary support through CSOs is less common than in other countries. However, recent changes in the management of Global Fund grants have started to expand the practice of onward granting through intermediaries, as well as the wider decentralization of funds through more CSOs.

CSOs play an essential prevention role. CSOs help address a crucial need in responding to the HIV epidemic in Peru, with most projects focused on prevention. Roughly one-third of CSO projects targeted key populations who are most-at-risk in Peru, including transgender people, MSM, and sex workers. In contrast, governmental prevention activities have not focused on prevention for these key populations.

The availability of data is good. Unlike in many other countries, Peru seems to have an extensive source of information on CSOs. This is the result of the legal requirement that ACPI record projects funded by external aid, which provides a complete information source for CSOs' own activities, budgets, and spending. Record keeping has been facilitated by the relatively small number of CSOs involved in HIV and AIDS activities.

Key Findings of Country Profiles

The three countries in this review present sharp differences in terms of their HIV epidemic, civil society involvement, the funding received by CSOs, and the assistance provided by the national AIDS responses.

HIV Epidemics
- India's HIV epidemic is concentrated within most-at-risk population groups and, while its overall adult prevalence rate is low (0.3 percent), some 2.4 million people are living with HIV and AIDS.
- Kenya has a mixed and heterogeneous generalized HIV epidemic (prevalence rate of 7.1 percent in 2007).
- Peru's epidemic is much more concentrated in some groups, and it has a much lower HIV prevalence rate (0.2 percent).

Civil Society Involvement
- India has a long tradition of supporting CSOs that operate at various levels. But, perhaps because of the importance of reaching high-risk groups, small NGOs and CBOs are much more at the core of India's AIDS response. They are viewed as essential for delivering targeted interventions to marginalized and hard-to-reach groups. Given the perceived crucial role of CSOs, more effort has been spent on ensuring that efficient programs are implemented and deliver results.
- Kenya has a long history of CSO activity and, as a result, CSOs are involved in the AIDS response at different levels of the society, including at community level. Until recently, however, their role was not perceived to be at the core of the response.
- Peru's CSOs have only recently become involved in HIV and AIDS response. There are a much more limited number of CSOs receiving AIDS funding, and it is only recently that CBOs are receiving funding for HIV and AIDS.

CSO Funding
- Both in Peru and Kenya, CSOs received little funding. However, the situation is changing—partly as a result of the recent changes in the Global Fund's management of grants. In the case of Kenya, the World Bank's HIV and AIDS project is providing increased funding, and an explicit role is being given to CSOs in KNASP III.
- In contrast, funding of India's civil society response represents a much larger share of the national response. This reflects the nature of India's epidemic and its AIDS response focused on delivering targeted interventions that are implemented by CSOs. As a result of strong donor support and government commitment, the funding for the community response represents at least 31 percent of the national HIV and AIDS funding.

Technical Assistance Provided to NGOs
- In Kenya and Nigeria, the main form of assistance is financial. Although the surveyed CBOs indicated that they spent resources on training, there were concerns that training was not of sufficient quality and not necessarily directed at improving the technical implementation capacity of CBOs.

- India, however, offers the example of a country where donors are encouraged to support a training fund aimed at providing technical assistance with the objective of strengthening the management capacity of CSOs and CBOs. In parallel, manuals and standards provide directions for the implementation of the targeted interventions by CBOs.

Strategic Choice
- The increase in the number and role of CSOs raises important issues. It is not always clear whether this increase is being pursued as an operational option for implementing donors' projects and objectives, or as a strategic policy choice resting on the strengths and limitations of the different types of CSOs (NGOs, CBOs, and FBOs).
- If civil society's contribution to the AIDS response is to become viable and strong, country-level support for managerial capacity building, organizational development, and human resource development have to be strengthened.
- One option is to transform small NGOs and CBOs into essential partners with performance-based contracting being a key component. Under this system, NGOs/CBOs would be contracted for implementing specific interventions and their contracts would be renewed provided the agreed-upon objectives have been met. At the same time, access to technical assistance would be provided to strengthen the management capacity of CSOs and CBOs.

Notes

1. See http://www.nacoonline.org/National_AIDS_Control_Program.
2. There is no single database of CSOs at national level. There are several databases of CSOs working on HIV and AIDS, but none are truly exhaustive.
3. For more information see http://www.nacoonline.org/Partnerships/Civil_Society.
4. This estimate excludes a funding gap of US$390 million for the period of NACP III.
5. This estimate excludes the funding gap of US$390 million both from the pool of funds and from the total resource envelope for NACP III.
6. Analysis of this system shows that it is used to improve results. As of December 2010, about 14 percent of the evaluated organizations did not pass the evaluation. Half of these had their contracts terminated while the others were put on a three month improvement plan.
7. See http://hivaidsclearinghouse.unesco.org/search/resources/5752_KenyaPlan2009.pdf.
8. In arriving at donor totals for this report, a few assumptions were made about individual entries and ultimate sources of funds. For instance, Family Health International and FACES were listed as donor agencies but likely received PEPFAR funds.
9. The amount of funding is relatively small because its use is limited to specific items. For instance, it cannot be used for paying wages.
10. On average CBOs employed 27 volunteers that did not receive compensation and 21 that did receive a compensation.

11. Reported as 110 million to 132 million nuevos soles per year in 2006–08, converted at 0.32 per U.S. dollar.
12. Other country-level spending (excluding management and human resources) included 18 percent for HIV research, 6 percent for enabling environment, 2 percent for social services and social protection, and 1 percent for orphans and vulnerable children.

References

Kenya. 2009. "Kenya National AIDS Spending Assessment. Report for the Financial Years 2006/07 and 2007/08." Kenya National AIDS Control Council, Nairobi.

Kenya CCM. 2007. *Kenya Round 7 Proposal in Response to Global Fund 7th Call for Proposals.* Nairobi: Kenya CCM.

Kenya National AIDS Control Council. 2010. "UNGASS 2010: United Nations General Assembly Special Session on HIV and AIDS, Country Report—Kenya." Kenya National AIDS Control Council, Nairobi.

Mohan, H. L., A. K. Blanchard, M. Shahmanesh, R. Prakash, S. Isac, B. M. Ramesh, P. Bhattacharjee, and S. Moses. 2011. *Evaluation of Community Mobilization and Empowerment in Relation to HIV Prevention among Female Sex Workers in Karnataka State, South India.* Bangalore, India: Karnataka Health Promotion Trust.

Peru Ministry of Health. 2008. *Informe Nacional sobre los Progresos Realizados en la Aplicación del UNGASS, Perú, periodo 2006–2007.* Lima: Peru Ministry of Health.

———. 2010. *Informe Nacional sobre los progresos realizados en la aplicación del UNGASS, Perú, Periodo: Enero 2008–Diciembre 2009.* Lima: Peru Ministry of Health.

Prinja, S., P. Bahuguna, S. Rudra, M. Kaur, S. M. Rehendete, S. Chatterjee, S. Panda, and R. Kumar. Sexually Transmitted Infections. 2011 Jun; 87(4): 354–61.

Saggurti, N., R. Manohar Mishra, L. Proddutoor, S. Tucker, D. Kovvali, P. Parimi, and T. Wheeler. 2011. *Community Collectivization and Its Association with Selected Outcomes among Female Sex Workes and High-Risk Men Who Have Sex with Men/Transgenders in Andhra Pradesh, India.* Washington, DC: World Bank.

UNAIDS (Joint United Nations Programme on HIV/AIDS). 2010. *What Countries Need; Investments Needed for 2010 Targets.* Geneva: UNAIDS.

Visser-Valfrey, M., R. Cassagnol, and M. Espinel. 2009. "UNAIDS Second Independent Evaluation, 2002–2008, Country Visit to Peru, Summary Report." UNAIDS, Geneva.

World Bank. 2011. *Effects of the Community Response to HIV and AIDS in Kenya.* Washington, DC: World Bank.

APPENDIX C

Survey of CSOs Involved in AIDS Responses

CSOs have become a mainstay of AIDS responses in most countries. The recent expansion of CSOs is the result of both civil societies' response to the HIV and AIDS epidemic and the large increase in international funding.[1] In this process, new financing systems have evolved and are shaping CSOs' institutional architecture.

The preceding analysis of funding flows from donors' perspectives, and the analysis of three countries highlighted how the available funding for the community response was being mobilized and used at country level. However, in nearly all cases, there was little information indicating how CSOs either funded their activities or allocated funding across activities. To shed some light on these issues, the HIV/AIDS Alliance obtained data from a survey of CSOs, which provided information on their activities and funding sources.

Responding Organizations

A confidential Internet-based survey was sent in 2010 to CSOs that work on AIDS in developing countries. A cascade method was used to target CSOs, by asking several international and regionally based organizations to directly e-mail their partner organizations and contacts. In addition, the survey was promoted generally through postings in e-forums and inclusion in electronic newsletters. To promote responses from locally based agencies, the survey was made available in English, French, Portuguese, Spanish, and Russian.

A total of 146 CSOs from around the world answered the online survey. National CSOs represented 89 percent of respondents, including 18 percent working at a national level and 71 percent working at subnational levels (that is, in local communities and districts).

Respondents were mainly from small and voluntary organizations: two-thirds had fewer than 20 staff members. They also relied on volunteers: 53 percent of the organizations had volunteers making up half or more of their workforce (figure C.1).

Figure C.1 Proportion of Volunteers in CSOs' Workforce
121 Respondents

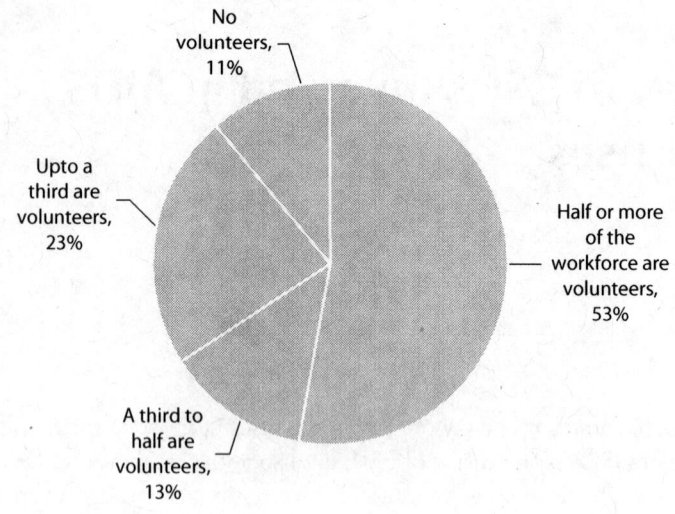

- No volunteers, 11%
- Upto a third are volunteers, 23%
- Half or more of the workforce are volunteers, 53%
- A third to half are volunteers, 13%

Source: International HIV/AIDS Alliance, survey 2010.

Figure C.2 Type of Organizations
Sample Size 121

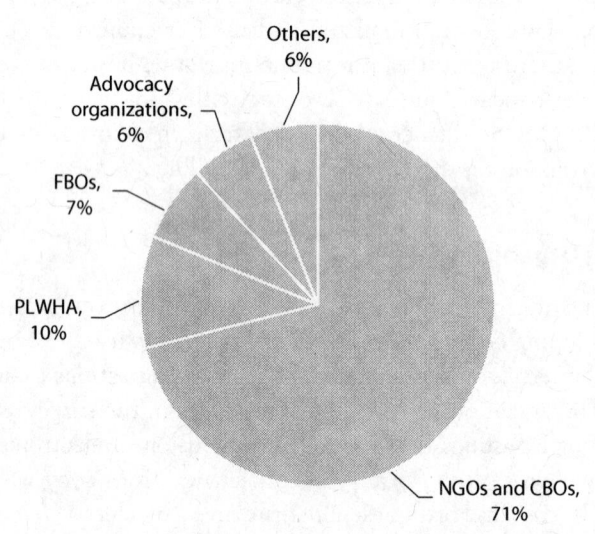

- Others, 6%
- Advocacy organizations, 6%
- FBOs, 7%
- PLWHA, 10%
- NGOs and CBOs, 71%

Source: International HIV/AIDS Alliance, survey 2010.

Almost three-quarters of the responding CSOs were NGOs or CBOs, and a tenth were peer-based organizations of people living with HIV. A smaller percentage were faith-based or advocacy organizations (figure C.2). More than half worked mainly on HIV and AIDS, but also on other development and health issues. Another 22 percent focused solely on HIV and AIDS, and 20 percent did some AIDS activities, but mostly worked in other development arenas.

Figure C.3 Geographic Location of CSOs
percentage of organizations; 112 respondents

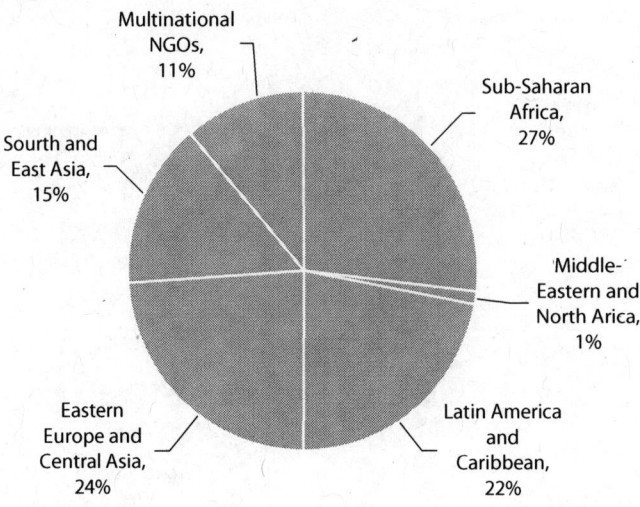

- Multinational NGOs, 11%
- Sub-Saharan Africa, 27%
- South and East Asia, 15%
- Middle-Eastern and North Arica, 1%
- Eastern Europe and Central Asia, 24%
- Latin America and Caribbean, 22%

Source: International HIV/AIDS Alliance, survey 2010.

The geographical origin of CSOs was diverse: 89 percent were in developing countries, but the geographical spread covered all regions. Some 27 percent of CSOs were located in Sub-Saharan Africa. Relatively large responses came from Latin America, Eastern Europe, and Central Asia (figure C.3).

Sources of Funding

Just over half of the CSOs surveyed indicated that they had two to four donors (figure C.4). More than a quarter received funding from a single donor, suggesting that these organizations were particularly exposed to funding variations.

The three sources of funding that respondents cited most often were the organization's own fund-raising, national funding mechanisms or government contracts, and foundations or charities. The fourth was the Global Fund.

More than half of the organizations indicated they relied on their own private fund-raising (figure C.5). Foundations and charities were an important source of funding for over 40 percent of the respondents, as were other country-level funding mechanisms (that is, government channels), which were also accessed by over 40 percent of the surveyed CSOs. Over one-third of the respondents indicated that they received funding from the Global Fund.

Relatively few CSOs were able to access direct funding provided by the U.S. Government agencies (CDC and USAID), DFID, and the World Bank HIV projects, but the percentage could be more significant than indicated in figure C.5. Survey responses could reflect two different situations: (1) the funding was underestimated because some passes through intermediaries such as

Figure C.4 Number of Institutional Donors
percent of organizations; 121 respondents

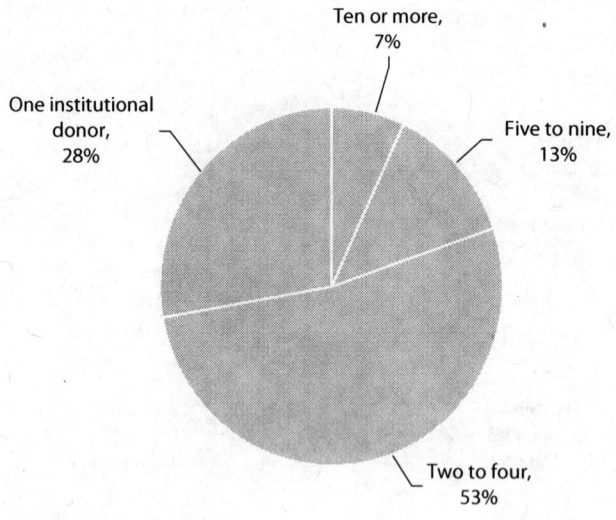

- One institutional donor, 28%
- Ten or more, 7%
- Five to nine, 13%
- Two to four, 53%

Source: International HIV/AIDS Alliance, survey 2010.

Figure C.5 Frequency of CSOs Receiving Funding from Each Source
121 respondents

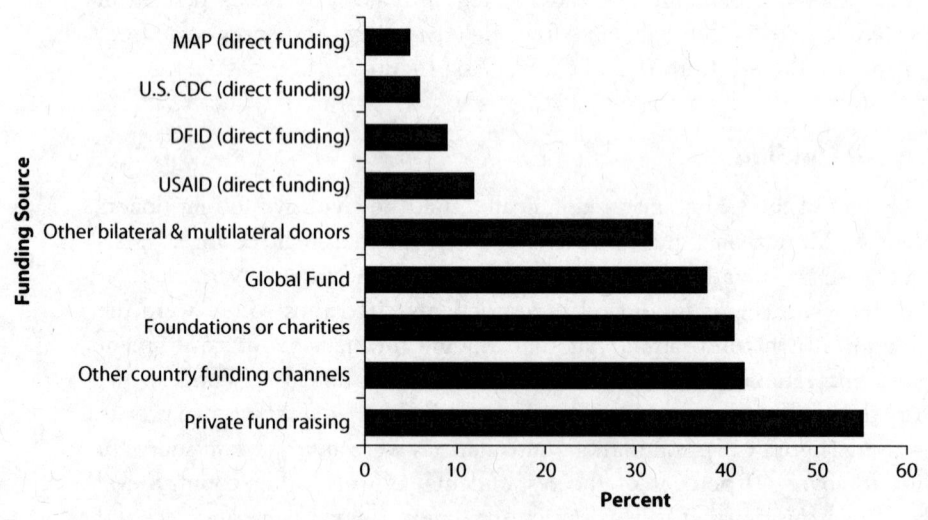

Funding Source (approximate percentages):
- MAP (direct funding): ~4%
- U.S. CDC (direct funding): ~6%
- DFID (direct funding): ~8%
- USAID (direct funding): ~12%
- Other bilateral & multilateral donors: ~32%
- Global Fund: ~37%
- Foundations or charities: ~41%
- Other country funding channels: ~42%
- Private fund raising: ~55%

Source: International HIV/AIDS Alliance, survey 2010.

large CSOs (in the case of U.S. Government agencies) and through national funding mechanisms (in the case of World Bank projects), or (2) the funding does not reach small CBOs working at the community level. Support for the first explanation is provided by the importance that respondents gave to country funding mechanisms (that is, funding provided through government channels).

Figure C.6 Average Distribution of Funding by Sources
percent of annual income; 121 respondents

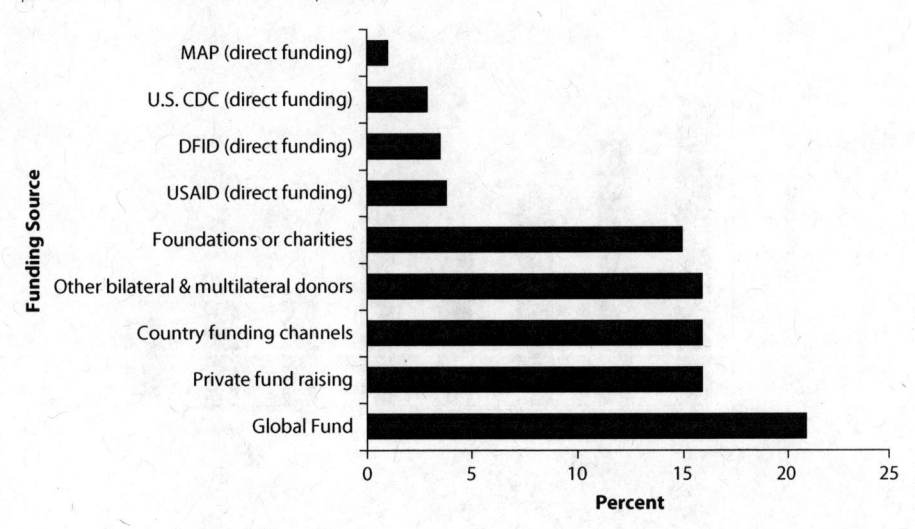

Funding Source	Percent
MAP (direct funding)	~1
U.S. CDC (direct funding)	~3
DFID (direct funding)	~3
USAID (direct funding)	~4
Foundations or charities	~15
Other bilateral & multilateral donors	~16
Country funding channels	~16
Private fund raising	~16
Global Fund	~21

Source: International HIV/AIDS Alliance, survey 2010.

Most Important Sources of Funding

The most important funding sources for the surveyed CSOs are shown in figure C.6. The Global Fund was the most important source, providing 21 percent of CSOs' revenues (this includes funding received as PRs (17 percent) and as sub-recipients (4 percent)). Three channels were nearly equal: foundations and charities, country funding mechanisms, and bilateral and multilateral donors.

Dominant Sources of Funding

In addition to the breakdown of funding by institutional sources, the survey also provided information on dominant funding sources, i.e., those that represent more than 50 percent of the respondents' annual budget. These results show that 21 percent of organizations report a diversified source of funding (figure C.7). The main dominant source of funding was the Global Fund, for 18 percent of the respondents. Overall, these data show an important degree of dependence on external sources of funding: perhaps as much as half the surveyed organizations may depend on a single dominant funder.

Expenditures on HIV and AIDS Activities

CSOs' largest annual expenditures, 42 percent on average, go toward prevention activities. Care and support represented almost 20 percent of annual expenditure on average, as did activities aimed at improving the enabling environment.

Figure C.7 Dominant Funding Sources
Percent of organizations with 50% or more from one source

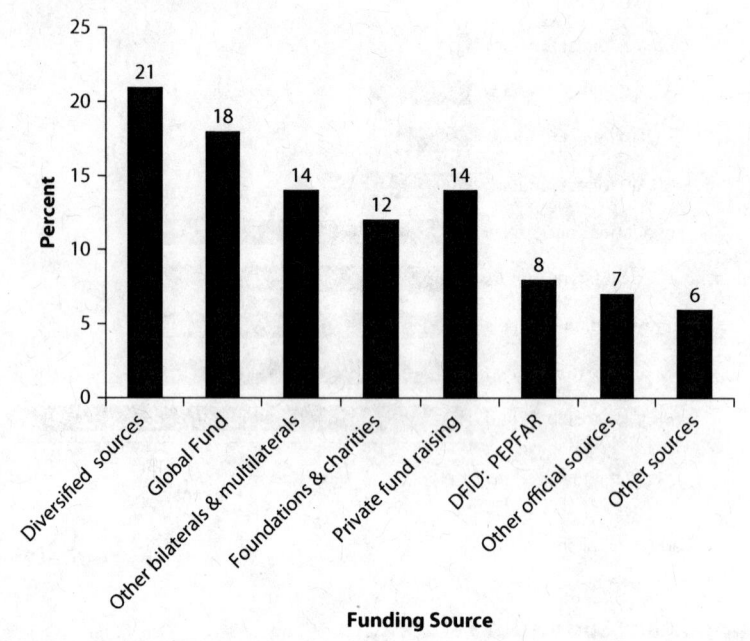

Funding Source	Percent
Diversified sources	21
Global Fund	18
Other bilaterals & multilaterals	14
Foundations & charities	12
Private fund raising	14
DFID: PEPFAR	8
Other official sources	7
Other sources	6

Source: International HIV/AIDS Alliance, survey 2010.

While major donor funding focuses on treatment, notably from PEPFAR and the Global Fund, survey respondents committed only 15 percent of annual expenditures, on average, to both treatment and support for treatment access and adherence. Finally, impact mitigation accounted, on average, for only 6 percent of annual expenditures (figure C.8).

The survey also asked for a further breakdown of spending within three categories.

- **Prevention**: Prevention expenditures were highest for activities reaching sex workers, MSM, IDUs, and people living with HIV and their partners (44 percent of prevention expenditures). Targeted prevention with populations such as women, youth, and migrants were the next highest expenditure. Together, these activities represented 71 percent of prevention expenditures. The rest went for awareness building and prevention activities targeted at the general population.
- **Treatment**: An average of 72 percent of treatment-related expenditure was used to support people living with HIV—for instance, help to gain access to clinical services or support to understand treatment adherence—rather than to actual drug procurement or provision (14 percent).
- **Care and support**: Expenditures were largely focused on people living with HIV (57 percent), with another 20 percent used for support to OVC and 10 percent for support to other adult family members.

Survey of CSOs Involved in AIDS Responses

Figure C.8 CSO Expenditures by Activities
103 respondents

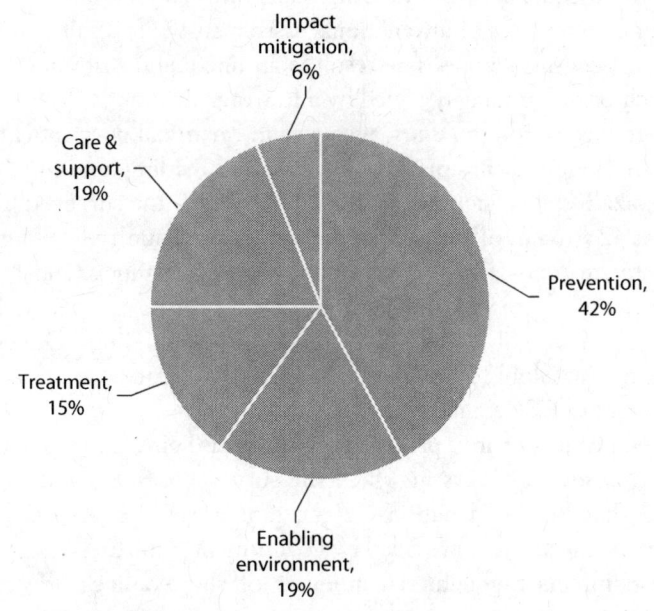

- Impact mitigation, 6%
- Care & support, 19%
- Prevention, 42%
- Treatment, 15%
- Enabling environment, 19%

Source: International HIV/AIDS Alliance, survey 2010.

Opinions about Funding, CSOs, and the AIDS Response

The survey also asked for opinions on specific issues. The answers relied on the views of participating individuals, but they provided insight into current thinking among CSOs. The most frequent reactions were the following:

- **More funding is needed:** 74 percent believed that more funding needs to be allocated to activities reaching vulnerable and most-at-risk populations.
- **The global economic crisis is affecting support:** 73 percent of those who expressed an opinion reported that there has been pressure on HIV budgets since the financial crisis started in 2009. On the other hand, 48 percent were "confident" that during the next five years donor funding for CSOs involved in HIV and AIDS activities will continue at the same level as now or will increase.
- **We are doing a good job:** CSO respondents were fairly confident in the quality of community action in their countries (64 percent agreed), but slightly over half (51 percent) were somewhat less confident about its comprehensiveness.
- **We need support for capacity building:** A majority (57 percent) reported that there was insufficient technical support and capacity development available to CSOs working on AIDS.
- **Partnership works, but could be better:** There was also relative confidence in collaboration among CSOs (59 percent agreed). However, 51 percent expressed somewhat reduced confidence in CSO-government collaboration.

Key Findings

- **CSOs have unequal access to funding.** Large international and national CSOs are the main recipients of international assistance, while small CBOs rely primarily on domestic sources. The result is an unequal distribution of funding, with much of the funding received by a few organizations.
- **The emergence of intermediary agencies and national government channels for transmitting funds has played a key role in providing funding to small and medium-sized CSOs, including CBOs.** On average the surveyed CSOs indicated that 42 percent of annual income came from country-level funding programs (private fund-raising, government funding channels, and foundations and charities).
- **CSOs remain heavily dependent on external funding.** Direct funding provided by the Global Fund and bilateral and multilateral sources amounted to 47 percent of CSOs' incomes.
- **CSO expenditures fit into profiles that confirm their complementary role in AIDS responses.** The ways in which the surveyed CSOs spent their money indicated that local and national organizations are delivering services that complement the services provided by government ministries.
- **CSO respondents highlighted a number of shortcomings affecting CSOs activities**
    - Seventy-five percent of the respondents felt that their HIV and AIDS budget was insufficient for adequately providing services to vulnerable groups and the most-at-risk populations.
    - Fifty-seven percent of the respondents were also concerned that the quality of the funding does not allow CSOs to provide what is needed at the community level, and that they do not have adequate access to technical assistance.

Note

1. For instance, in the six Sub-Saharan African countries that Birdsall and Kelly (2007) reviewed, total CSO spending on AIDS tripled between 2001 and 2005. This is based on a study of 439 CSOs.

References

Birdsall, K., and K. Kelly. 2007. *Pioneers, Partners, Providers: The Dynamics of Civil Society and AIDS Funding in Southern Africa.* Johannesburg: Centre for AIDS Development, Research and Evaluation CADRE/Open Society Initiative for Southern Africa.

APPENDIX D

OSISA-CADRE Survey of CSOs Working on HIV and AIDS

This appendix, which is adapted with minor changes from Olivier and Wodon (2011a, 2011b), provides an analysis of data collected by Birdsall and Kelly (2007) from CSOs in six southern African countries (Lesotho, Malawi, Mozambique, Namibia, Swaziland, and Zambia). The objective of this exercise was to assess to what extent CSOs have benefited from increased funding for HIV-AIDS over the period 2000–05, as well as how they have used the funds received and whether they have become vulnerable to cuts in funding. While Birdsall and Kelly focused on the broader CSO landscape, this study assessed the comparative characteristics and funding patterns of faith-based CSOs (FB-CSOs) as compared to nonreligious or secular CSOs (S-CSOs).

Responding Organizations

The survey consisted of a four-page questionnaire that was sent to samples of relatively well-established CSOs working on the AIDS response in Lesotho, Malawi, Mozambique, Namibia, Swaziland, and Zambia. A list of CSOs working on HIV and AIDS was created in each country using information from AIDS coordination networks, National AIDS Coordinating Authorities (NACAs), and institutions providing grants and sub-grants. In the dataset provided by the authors of the original study, data were available on 368 organizations. This analysis is based on 349 organizations out of the 369 because only those organizations that stated whether they were faith-based in orientation or not were included (there were 20 missing values). Out of the 349 organizations, 117 were FB-CSOs and 232 were S-CSOs.

In most cases, there were relatively few differences in the characteristics of S-CSOs and FB-CSOs. For both groups, 55 percent of the CSOs were located in a town or city that is an administrative center for surrounding areas or towns, versus 45 percent in a rural village or small town. For both groups, close to 75 percent worked in more than one community. The CSOs had a similar background with respect to the number of years they had existed and the number of years they had worked on HIV-AIDS. Approximately 40 percent of the organizations were created since 2001 and close to 60 percent started to work on HIV-AIDS in later years.

There are a few areas where one observes differences between the two types of CSOs. FB-CSOs tended to be slightly more international, more connected to other organizations working on HIV and AIDS, and active in other areas than was the case for S-CSOs.[1] Another difference is that, as expected, S-CSOs tended to have a higher ratio of paid staff (full-time or part-time) to the number of volunteers working for the organization than was the case for FB-CSOs. This was true for both national and international staff.

In relation to CSOs' HIV and AIDS activities, the FB-CSOs surveyed were somewhat more active in treatment, care, support, and impact mitigation than was the case for S-CSOs. By contrast, S-CSOs were slightly more active in prevention, as well as in policy, advocacy, and research. But, overall, differences in activity profiles tended to be small.

The survey also asked CSOs which target groups they served. At least two features of the data stood out. First, in general, FB-CSOs served a larger number of target groups than was the case with S-CSOs. This finding may be related to the fact that FB-CSOs were more likely to run other programs and were, thus, able to provide services to more target groups than was the case for S-CSOs. (This comment should not be interpreted as FB-CSOs necessarily serving more persons, rather, that they served more varied target groups).

Main Sources of Funding

Table D.1 provides selected data on expenditures and funding for the period 2001–05. First, it is clear that average levels of spending on HIV and AIDS among the CSOs in the sample have increased sharply over time, with the corresponding amounts for both groups being almost three times higher in 2005 than in 2001. Second, the average funding per CSO is substantial (US$160,000 per S-CS0 and US$150,000 per FB-CSOs). This suggests that the sample includes mostly established organizations, as opposed to local and more informally run CBOs, which would have much smaller budgets.

The survey also asked whether the CSOs benefited from funding from specific types of donors. Instead of presenting data on the percentage of organizations that benefited from a specific funding source, these percentages have been scaled into indices, with the likelihood of a S-CSO benefitting from funding from a foreign donor or an international institution used as the baseline. The data on funding source by type are, thus, interpreted as relative odds ratios with the comparison being international donor funding in 2001 for S-CSOs. Three main observations can be made from this analysis. First, the odds ratios were systematically higher in 2005 than they were in 2001, indicating that funding has increased for all types of donors. Second, the largest increase in funding over time has been from national, provincial, or district HIV and AIDS structures.

Table D.1 Expenditure Levels and Types of Organizations Funding CSOs

	2001	2002	2003	2004	2005
S-CSOs					
Average total expenditure on HIV and AIDS (US$)	49,201	69,763	94,175	121,892	160,141
Number of grants from different sources	1.80	—	2.15	—	2.68
* Foreign donor or international institution	1.00	1.01	1.08	1.08	1.10
* Government department or ministry	0.57	0.63	0.76	0.76	0.77
* National, provincial or district HIV/AIDS structure	0.24	0.45	0.91	0.97	1.04
* Other NGO	0.62	0.73	0.87	0.99	1.04
* Services provided (fees from users)	0.71	0.75	0.86	0.89	0.90
* Local sources (businesses, churches, or charities)	0.77	0.83	0.86	0.91	0.95
FB-CSOs					
Total expenditure on HIV and AIDS (US$)	56,642	63,932	104,296	133,818	150,613
Number of grants from different sources	1.63	—	2.18	—	2.89
* Foreign donor or international institution	1.06	1.07	1.08	1.09	1.12
* Government department or ministry	0.68	0.68	0.91	0.85	0.96
* National, provincial or district HIV/AIDS structure	0.38	0.83	0.91	0.94	1.03
* Other NGO	0.91	0.95	0.98	1.03	1.11
* Services provided (fees from users)	0.97	1.00	1.00	1.04	1.04
* Local sources (businesses, churches, or charities)	0.94	0.97	1.02	1.02	1.04

Source: Olivier and Wodon 2011b using CADRE database.
Note: * Indicates that the variable is expressed as an index value; see text for explanation. — = Not available.

Third, FB-CSOs tended to report slightly different funding sources than was the case for S-CSOs.

Another question related to the type of funding received by class of expenditure (table D.2). Again, the differences between FB-CSOs and S-CSOs were limited, even though FB-CSOs tended to have a higher likelihood of benefitting from funding than S-CSOs. Not surprisingly, the category least eligible for funding was equipment or vehicles. The other three categories—salary, administrative, and program costs—were equally likely to be supported by external

Table D.2 External Financial Assistance by Type of Expenditure (%)

	No funding	Some funding	Full funding	All
S-CSOs				
Salaries, stipends, or incentives	45.8	31.8	22.4	100
Office and administration costs	37.1	42.3	20.6	100
Program costs, including supplies	42.3	38.0	19.8	100
Equipment or vehicles	61.6	18.6	19.8	100
FB-CSOs				
Salaries, stipends, or incentives	36.2	44.7	19.3	100
Office and administration costs	29.4	39.7	30.9	100
Program costs, including supplies	24.7	52.6	22.7	100
Equipment or vehicles	59.3	26.7	14.0	100

Source: Olivier and Wodon 2011b using CADRE database.

Table D.3 Success Rates in Funding Proposals and Dependency on Funding (%)

	Number of proposals for funding			Activities driven by funding opportunities			
	Prepared	Response	Approved	Not at all	A little	Very much	All
S-CSO	5.0	2.9	1.6	9.9	25.6	64.6	100
FB-CSO	6.8	3.5	1.9	10.8	25.2	64.0	100

Source: Olivier and Wodon 2011b using CADRE database.

Table D.4 Perspectives on Budgets and Funding Security (%)

	Perspectives on budget			Share of funding needed secured for next year			
	Donor's priorities	New funding	Cuts in programs	0–25%	26–50%	51–75%	76–100%	All
S-CSO	45.79	29.55	63.18	45.23	24.12	20.6	10.05	100
FB-CSO	42.53	33.64	57.8	43.69	20.39	23.3	12.62	100

Source: Olivier and Wodon 2011b using CADRE database.

assistance. (One might have expected that program costs would be more likely to be funded than administration, but this does not appear to be the case.)

In table D.3, the number of grant proposals submitted by FB-CSOs was higher than for S-CSOs (6.8 proposals versus 5.0). The success rate for proposals was slightly higher for S-CSOs at 33 percent versus 27 percent for FB-CSOs. As to whether the activities run by the CSOs were driven by donor funding, close to two-thirds of both types of CSOs indicated that this was very much the case, versus 10 percent stating not at all.

Four additional questions from the survey are reported in table D.4. The first question was whether CSOs felt that donor priorities for funding have changed. Almost half of the CSOs stated that this was the case. The second question was whether CSOs have started new programs mainly because funding was offered for those activities; about one-third of the organizations stated that this was the case. The third question was whether CSOs have cut back on any areas of activity because of absence of funding. Approximately 60 percent responded in the affirmative, which suggests that, while funding has indeed increased, there were also clear limitations set on the available funding. Finally, CSOs were asked about the proportion of their planned program that was already funded for the next 12 months. In many cases, the proportion seemed rather small, which suggests a high level of vulnerability (of both types of CSOs) to any decrease in HIV and AIDS funding.

Key Findings

- The evidence to date on whether different types of CSOs have been able to access various sources of funding for HIV and AIDS has been limited. Analysis of the survey implemented by Birdsall and Kelly (2007) suggests that, among formal and relatively well-established CSOs working on HIV and AIDS in

developing countries, donor funding has increased and is now significant. It has also enabled the CSOs to expand their activities. The profile of relatively well-established FB-CSOs and S-CSOs (those most likely to be included in this dataset) is rather similar—in terms of the areas on which they work, their sources of funding and their levels of expenditure.
- The scaled-up response to HIV and AIDS from CSOs has been observed across the full range of CSOs—from formal national-scale CSOs and networks to the proliferation of new community-level initiatives and programs, and among both faith-based and secular organizations. While some of these initiatives emerged as a response to need, many appeared as a result of the greatly increased availability of HIV and AIDs funding over that period. In today's context, where funding for HIV and AIDS is becoming scarcer, questions about whether newly created CSOs will be able to survive, or how their resources might be "redirected" so that their capacity and experience is not lost, remains worryingly unclear.

Note

1. The proportion of FB-CSOs that have branches or programs in other countries, at 18 percent, is higher than for S-CSOs, at 10 percent. And the proportion of FB-CSOs that are part of an HIV/AIDS association or coordinating network/body is also slightly higher for FB-CSOs, at 90 percent, versus 83 percent for S-CSOs. Also, 72 percent of FB-CSOs conduct activities not related to HIV/AIDS, versus 64 percent of S-CSOs.

References

Birdsall, K., and K. Kelly. 2007. *Pioneers, Partners, Providers: The Dynamics of Civil Society and AIDS Funding in Southern Africa*. Johannesburg: Centre for AIDS Development, Research and Evaluation CADRE/Open Society Initiative for Southern Africa.

Olivier, J., and Q. Wodon. 2011a. *Layers of Evidence: Discourses and Typologies on Faith-Inspired Community Responses to HIV/AIDS in Africa, Mimeo*. Washington, DC: World Bank.

———. 2011b. *Faith-inspired Funding? Funding Stream for Community HIV/AIDS Response in Africa, Mimeo*. Washington, DC: World Bank.

APPENDIX E

Consultative Process

This paper benefited from a consultative process carried out with the UK Consortium for AIDS and International Development that included specialists, CSOs, and development partners. This paper builds on a preliminary report prepared for the World Bank by the following staff at the International AIDS Alliance: Aurora Riva Patrón, Peru; Meera Mishra, India; Urbanus Mutuku Kioko, Kenya; Liza Tong, UK; Julia Ross, UK; and Sarah Owen, UK.

The authors wish to thank and acknowledge the following reviewers for providing useful comments and insights on previous versions of this paper:

Katie Bigmore, Anne Bossuyt, Carmen Carpio, Mariam Claeson, Michael Dwyer, John Garrison, Joana Godinho, Eva Jarawan, Anderson Stanciole, Tony Thompson, Quentin Wodon—World Bank

Hernan Rosenberg—Pan American Health Organization

Katja Roll—The Global Fund to Fight AIDS, Tuberculosis, and Malaria

Lois Chingandu—SAfAIDS, South Africa

Denise Hunt—The AIDS Consortium, South Africa

Titus James Twesige—The Eastern Africa National Networks of AIDS Service Organizations (EANNASO), Tanzania

Lydia Mungherera—The AIDS Support Organisation (TASO), Uganda

Ben Simms and Nigel Thompson—UK Consortium for AIDS and International Development

Christy Abraham—Action AIDS International, India

Do Dang Dong—Vietnamese National Network of PLHIV (VNP+)

Alessandra Nilo—Latin America and the Caribbean Council of AIDS Service Organizations (LACCASO)

Nigel Taylor—Thembisa Development Consulting

Shannon Hayes—Huarou Commission, United States

A special thank you goes to Uma Balasubramanian and Mario Mendez, HNP, World Bank, for the invaluable administrative support provided to the evaluation team.

Any error or omission in the paper is that of the authors only and does not implicate in any way the above individuals who graciously provided feedback and advice.